PLATO':
THE 'INDE

MW00881037

Also by A. P. David

Non-Fiction
> *The Dance of the Muses: Choral Theory and Ancient Greek Poetics*

> (Web resources: http://danceofthemuses.org)

Fiction
> *'I am a Forgotten Man': Yuri's Odyssey*

> *The Tale of the Pig Man* or *'Waking Up'*

Poetry
> *Past Your Ear*

Plato's New Measure

The 'Indeterminate Dyad'

A. P. David

Mother Pacha, Inc.
Austin, Texas

All Rights Reserved. No part of this book may be used or reproduced in any manner whatsoever without written permission except in the case of brief quotations embodied in critical articles or reviews.

Copyright © 2011 by A. P. David

Published by Mother Pacha, Inc.
315 W. 37th Street
Austin, Texas 78705
USA

ISBN-13: 978-1466383982
ISBN-10: 1466383984

for John White

... συλλαβεῖν εἰς ἕν ...

Preface

The seed of this monograph was sown one lunch period in a December nearly thirty years ago, during my freshman year at St. John's College. My Euclid tutor John White, later a colleague, took me aside, at my request, for some extra intellectual stimulus that my class could not then provide. He taught me about *anthyphairesis*, the ancient method of measurement through mutual subtraction. I remember in equal parts the fascination with the concept and the privilege of receiving such attention from 'Mr. White'. John is an exceptional teacher and as patient a man as one could find.

The idea lay fallow until one glorious spring day almost at the end of my senior year, when the late David Fowler (of the University of Warwick) visited the campus. He gave a talk on the possibility of 'same *anthyphairesis*' being a way of defining 'same ratio', a way which appeared in fact to be standard for the pre-Euclidean Aristotle. We spent the day talking and watching a tour-de-force puppet rendition of ancient comedy. He gave me some pointers and references, and when I arrived in Chicago for graduate school I checked almost every day in the library catalogue to see if his book had come out. (It was at least a year delayed.) When, many years later, I finally thought to thank him for that inspiration and that afternoon, alas I discovered he had passed away.

The first versions of these two chapters were delivered as presentations to the Ancient Philosophy Workshop at the University of Chicago, then led in the late '80s and early '90s by Ian Mueller and Arthur W. H. Adkins. They were finally published, separately, in the *St. John's Review* in the early 2000s. Unfortunately the printing of the second paper skipped the footnotes. The current monograph is not so much revised from those papers, as cleaned up and organized. It is happy for me, however, to see them at last as the one treatment that they are.

I was not happy with the way philosophy departments treat Plato, and besides, by the time I finished this project, the late Plato did not seem all that far from a Cartesian, in certain important aspects. That put me off. I had thought in the ancient world I was on to something different. I much prefer the Plato who dramatized Socrates, as perhaps did the man himself. Certainly he preserved his early writings; I feel sure that all of them were left polished as he wanted, 'even afterward'. Thus the very act of producing this monograph led me to focus rather on Homer and philology. So why knock on the door of a professional philosophy journal or publisher? A scholar, unlike a student, ought to be his own judge, not a pawn of 'peers' and tenure. I am a joyful amateur.

So in hopes that whatever insight is here will find its way to fruitful soil, I send this piece on its way to fare on its own. What there is here of reconstruction of history (or intellectual history), about Plato's so-called Academy and other matters, is not drawn from modern assumptions, external commentary, or centuries-after-the-fact anecdote; it is drawn, rather, from inference from the texts themselves of Plato and Aristotle. This delights me. Draw the figures in the sand, if there is no chalkboard! Or on the chalkboard in your mind. The 'indeterminate dyad' has been a mysterious thing almost since its conception. Plato himself never used the term in extant writing. It turns out to be a simple and illuminating kind of algorithm which unmasks something masked, it seems to me, by the modern calculus and the number-line.

A. P. David
Austin, Texas
October 2011

Contents

Plato's New Measure
The 'Indeterminate Dyad'

Chapter 1

The Paradigms of Theaetetus

A fresh interpretation of the geometry lesson (Theaetetus 147c-148b) and its significance for Plato's development

I find the grounds for a new reconstruction of Theodorus' geometry lesson (*Theaetetus* 147c-148b) in the detail of Plato's prose. In this chapter I shall first present this reconstruction, and then discuss the significance of the mathematics involved in Theaetetus' solution to Theodorus' problem, both in itself and for the development of Plato's later philosophy—nothing less than a revolution in his thought—which is represented by the sequence of dialogues *Theaetetus, Sophist,* and *Politicus.*

A. *The Lesson*

Early in the *Theaetetus* Socrates has already raised the animating question of the dialogue: what is knowledge? Theaetetus answers by pointing to different types and objects of knowledge, such as the things Theodorus knows (geometry) and the knowledge of craftsmen (146c). We did not want to count its sorts and objects, says Socrates (146e), but to find out what 'knowledge' itself is. He adds that if one does not know what the word 'clay' refers to, if it is a mere name, there could be no illumination in defining it as oven-maker's clay and brick-maker's clay. Besides, the simple answer to 'what is clay?' would be earth mixed with water (147c). Perhaps Socrates is asking for an account that connects a name to a nature. At any rate, Theaetetus thinks he has just encountered an example of such a thing in the course of a lesson given by Theodorus, to him and his young friend also called Socrates. (Theaetetus *looks* like the famous Socrates; young Socrates bears his *name*; there is a third companion and fellow wrestler mentioned (144c), who remains an unknown.) What Theaetetus had done in response to the lesson of Theodorus was to come up with new names—or rather, to apply old names in a new way—so as to demarcate for the first time two different kinds of square roots (and, as we shall see in the next chapter, a third kind by implication).

Some heretofore neglected particles occur in Theaetetus' description of Theodorus' lesson; here is John McDowell's translation:

Θε: Περὶ δυνάμεών τι ἡμῖν Θεόδωρος ὅδε ἔγραφε τῆς τε τρίποδος πέρι καὶ πεντέποδος ἀποφαίνων ὅτι μήκει οὐ σύμμετροι τῇ ποδιαίᾳ, καὶ οὕτω κατὰ μίαν ἑκάστην προαιρούμενος μέχρι τῆς ἑπτακαιδεκάποδος.

Theaetetus: Theodorus here was drawing diagrams to show us something about powers—namely that a square of three square feet and one of five square feet aren't commensurable, in respect of length of side, with a square of one square foot; and so on, selecting each case individually, up to seventeen square feet.

Note that 'powers' is misleading here. Wilbur Knorr points out that δύναμις and δυνάμει mean 'square' and 'in square' throughout Greek mathematical literature, including in Hippocrates of Chios, who was a contemporary of Theodorus and Theaetetus; he shows that Plato also uses the terms consistently in this sense, citing the *Republic* 587d, *Timaeus* 54b, and *Politicus* 266b.[1] Since Theaetetus' peculiar appropriation and application of the term occurs later in the passage, one may conclude that Theodorus' demonstration had to do with squares.

The use of τε-καὶ in Greek composition signals a grouping by the composer; the paired elements in this case are τῆς τρίποδος (the square of three feet) and πεντέποδος (the square of five feet). The balance and symmetry of the formulation, τῆς τε τρίποδος πέρι καὶ πεντέποδος, with περί accented in postposition, seems to suggest a natural balance in the flanking elements. I was led to wonder, could there be something special about this

---

[1]Wilbur R. Knorr, *Evolution of the Euclidean Elements*, Dordrecht and Boston: D. Reidel Pub. Co., 1975, 65-9

pair of squares in the context of Theodorus' investigation? Since he takes up each square individually (κατὰ μίαν ἑκάστην), is there a reason why these two are paired? On reading the linking particles with their natural sense, the connecting phrase καὶ οὕτω shades into a non sequitur: after proving something about a pair of squares, Theodorus 'in this way' selects each square individually. But if this pair served as paradigms for the later squares, a better sense can be given to καὶ οὕτω ... προαιρούμενος: once he had proved something about two paradigm cases, Theodorus could thereby pick out in advance (προαιρέομαι) each succeeding case, reducing them one by one to either of the paradigm cases, up to the seventeen-foot square. This reading would be consistent with Plato's phrasing: ἔγραφε ἀποφαίνων governs only the three- and five-foot squares, about which (περί) Theodorus would have pictorially demonstrated something, and προαιρούμενος covers each of the following cases, which he would have only needed to 'pick out'.

A simpler reading of καὶ οὕτω would suggest that Theodorus covered only the odd number squares: having started with three and five, he continues this way in order (the series being three, five, seven, etc.). Certainly, the sense of προαιρέομαι only demands that there be *some* kind of advance selection involved, whether the cases of three and five formed a paradigmatic basis for the selection or merely established a pattern of successive odd numbers. It may also be that the criterion of selection preceded and included three and five, not as analytic paradigms but simply as first cases; perhaps Theodorus was picking out individual numbers because they were *already* known or intuited to have incommensurable roots, and the object of his lesson was to offer proofs of the fact. On this reading, one would need to explain why he omitted the case of two. But on this reading as well, and indeed on any other, one must still ask why three and five should be paired off; and we observe that only in these two cases is there an explicit reference to the giving of proofs.

The next sentence in the passage has caused a lot of trouble, most recently in the unfriendly debate between Knorr and Miles Burnyeat in the pages of *Isis*.[2]

> ἐν δὲ ταύτῃ πως ἐνέσχετο.
> At that point he somehow got tied up.

The question comes to this: did Theodorus get 'tangled up' in the case of the seventeen-foot square, or did he merely stop (for some reason or no reason) at that one? Inference from the many examples in the lexicon under ἐνέχομαι suggests the former, but Burnyeat, following Mansfield, argues that instances of this word which mean 'get entangled' furnish in context an explicit cause for the difficulty.[3] Knorr's reconstruction of the proofs, by means of Pythagorean triangles and number triples,

> ... entails the division of the problem into classes of numbers, represented by the numbers 3, 5, 6, and 17. Each class requires a treatment differing from the others. But the method, successful for the former

---

[2]Wilbur R. Knorr and Miles F. Burnyeat, 'Methodology, Philology, and Philosophy', *Isis*, 1979, 70:565-70

[3]Miles Burnyeat, 'The Philosophical Sense of Theaetetus' Mathematics', *Isis*, 1978, 69:489-513, 513

classes, fails at 17.[4]

Burnyeat rejects this reconstruction, and the reading of πως ἐνέσχετο that it implies, because he sees no evidence for the treatment by classes in the text. My reading would help to supply that evidence: the cases of three and five could be seen as paradigmatic for the other cases, representing in Knorr's scheme all numbers of the form (4N+3) and (8N+5).

There is no evidence, however, for treatment by *four* classes. The class of numbers represented by six in Knorr's solution need not have been part of Theodorus' lesson as it is described in the text; we hear only of three, odd-number examples (and this may in itself be evidence that Theodorus only covered the odd numbers). It is perhaps a weakness of Knorr's reconstruction that the number seventeen does not fall into either of the classes represented by three and five, but is made to represent a separate class. It is a strength, however, that it shares this class (8N+1) with all the odd square numbers (nine,

---

[4]Knorr, *Evolution*, 192

twenty-five, etc.); Knorr suggests that the failure of the method in this case is what led Theaetetus to a new approach, precisely via the distinction between square and non-square numbers.[5]

There is a serious objection to Knorr's approach, however. His proofs of root-incommensurability for the classes (4N+3) and (8N+5) do not themselves depend on the proofs for three and five; the general cases must be proved independently, with a dose of algebraic manipulation. Indeed, if Knorr wants to avoid the worst kind of anachronism, involving the use of zero, the cases of three and five (N=0) must be specifically excluded from the proofs. There is no hint in the text, however, of this kind of generalization. My reading allows only that the individual, concrete proofs for three and five may have been the paradigms for the later cases. The generality would in that case have to be contained in these very proofs.

Knorr argues cogently that περὶ δυνάμεών τι ... ἔγραφε means that Theodorus 'proved something [about

---

[5]Ibid.

squares] by means of diagrams', rather than that he merely drew the squares or that he only proved something about them.[6] Where moderns are accustomed to express the generality of arithmetical solutions through algebraic formulae, those Greek mathematicians whose work culminates in Euclid appear to have used geometrical diagrams in this capacity, as themselves the immediate means to convey the universality of a proposition, including in arithmetic or number theory. I therefore sought something in the structure of the possible diagrams for proving incommensurability of the side in the cases of the three- and the five-foot square that made them each essentially paradigmatic. The reconstruction requires successful proofs which suggest through the generality of their diagrams an applicability to an infinite number of cases, but which appear to involve a difficulty in the case of the seventeen-foot square.

The solution was surprisingly forthcoming: it requires but two, simple theorems, one for each paradigm

---

[6]Ibid., 69 ff.

case, which fall out from the Pythagorean dot-arithmetic (also reconstructed in our time, with considerable elegance, by Knorr); and it satisfies all interpretations of the activity implied by γράφειν. In fact, each of Knorr's own criteria for a reconstruction of the lesson is met most elegantly by this method.[7]

I constructed the roots by using pairs of successive integers, starting with the unit, following Malcolm Brown's lead.[8] When each of these pairs—{1,2}, {2,3}, {3,4}, etc.—is taken as leg and hypotenuse of a right triangle, the desired sequence of squares, equal to the sequence of odd numbers, is produced on the remaining (in this case, left-

---

[7]Ibid., 96 (In full: '(a) The proofs are demonstrably valid. (b) The treatment by special cases and the stopping *at* 17 are necessitated by the methods of proof employed. (c) The proofs will be understood to apply to an infinite number of cases. (d) No use may be made of the dichotomy of square and oblong numbers in Theodorus' studies, either in the demonstrations or in the choice of cases to be treated. (e) Theodorus' proofs utilize the special relations of the lines in the construction of the *dynameis*. The geometrical methods of construction are of the type characteristic of metrical geometry as developed in *Elements* II and are closely associated with a certain early style of arithmetic theory. (f) But the arithmetic methods by which Theaetetus could prove the two general theorems, on the incommensurability of lines associated with non-square and non-cubic integers, were not available to Theodorus.'

[8]Malcolm Brown, 'Theaetetus: Knowledge as Continued Learning', *Journal of the History of Philosophy*, 1969, 7:359-79, 367-8

hand) legs:

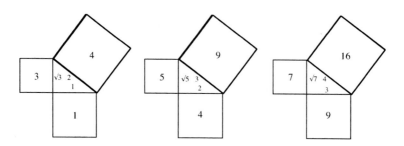

The odd numbers therefore form a kind of natural sequence in their square representations: they can be understood as the first 'offspring' in two dimensions of the natural numbers in one, when these are successively 'mated' by means of right triangles. The objection that the text seems to say that Theodorus proved something about squares in general—and hence an assumption in reconstructions that he covered the case of six and a puzzle as to why he left out two—can be met by considering that in the context of a Pythagorean geometrical arithmetic, the odds beginning with three form a distinct and natural genetic grouping among the square versions of numbers. Three is in fact the *first*

square produced in this configuration of the famous triangle—not two—by the sequence of natural numbers expressed as lengths, beginning with the unit length; and five is the second. The text bears without strain the sense of a movement from general to specific. Theodorus proved something about squares: *namely*, about that natural sequence of squares which begins with three and five, *that* a selection of them are incommensurable with the unit length. Moreover, the allusive quality of the description, which has fostered so many modern attempts at interpretation, would suit an association with a well-known Pythagorean construction such as the one drawn above.

The three-foot and five-foot squares are the first two constructed by means of these pairs of the natural numbers. The form of proof is reduction to absurdity. Take the first case: the side of the three-foot square (or the 'three-foot side') must be either commensurable or incommensurable with the side of the unit square (or 'unit side'). Assume it commensurable. Then there exists some ratio of numbers, A:B, between the three-foot side and the unit side. Take this ratio in its lowest terms; then either A is odd and B is even, or B is odd and A is even, or both are odd. But the hypotenuse is even:

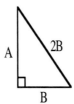

Therefore both A and B must be even (by Knorr's Theorem V.14 about Pythagorean triples).[9] Hence either A or B or both must be odd and even simultaneously, which is an impossible situation for a number. The three-foot side and the unit side cannot, therefore, have the ratio of a number to a number, and they are incommensurable.[10]

The generalization immediately follows from the diagram: all of the roots constructed by a triangle with an even hypotenuse—that is, constructed by the pairs $\{1,2\}$, $\{3,4\}$, $\{5,6\}$, $\{7,8\}$, etc. yielding $\sqrt{3}$, $\sqrt{7}$, $\sqrt{11}$, $\sqrt{15}$, etc. on the remaining legs—generate the same paradox (that a

[9]Knorr, *Evolution*, 158

[10]This proof is given by Knorr, *Evolution*, 184

number must be simultaneously odd and even) if they are assumed to be commensurable with the unit side. Each of these triangles has the following paradigmatic form in the diagram drawn in the course of the proof, on the assumption that there is some numerical ratio A:B between the root and the unit:

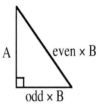

The five-foot square, constructed by means of a triangle with an odd hypotenuse, presents the only alternative paradigm produced by these numerical pairs:

The right-hand figure represents the numerical relations

between the sides of the triangles in the proofs for all the cases involving an odd hypotenuse—that is, those triangles built with the pairs {2,3}, {4,5}, {6,7}, etc., yielding $\sqrt{5}$, $\sqrt{9}$, $\sqrt{13}$, etc. on the remaining legs. In each case, assume that the particular root is commensurable with the unit. Then it has a ratio of a number to a number with the unit side, A:B. In lowest terms, one or both of these numbers is odd. If B is even, the hypotenuse is even, and so A would also be even, as before; hence B must be odd. Then A must also be odd, since it is a given that the other leg is even; if A were even, the two even squares on the legs would equal the odd square on the hypotenuse, which is impossible. But if A is odd, the square on the remaining (bottom) leg must be equal to a difference of odd squares. *This could only be true if it were a multiple of eight.*[11] A square that is a multiple of eight is also a multiple of sixteen. It must therefore have a side that is a multiple of four. Since B is odd, this side is equal to a rectangular number, (even) × (odd), and the (even) side must itself be a multiple of four, if the whole number is

---

[11]Ibid., 159

also to be a multiple of four. We must therefore pick out and examine each of the relevant cases in turn, to see if the even member of the number-pairs is a multiple of four. If not, the condition is not met, A can be neither odd nor even, and there can be no ratio of numbers A:B such that the respective side is commensurable with the unit side. In the case of {2,3} and the five-foot square, for example, we find the condition unmet, since two is not a multiple of four: the five-foot side is therefore proved incommensurable with the unit side. In the next case—the nine-foot square constructed by the pair {4,5}—the condition *is* in fact met, and the nine-foot side (i.e., three) happens to be commensurable. Meanwhile, the side of the thirteen-foot square, constructed by the pair {6,7}, is proved incommensurable, for six is not a multiple of four.

This establishes the paradigmatic nature of the two proofs and their diagrams. The cases of three and five involve the only two kinds of triangle produced by the constructing number-pairs: those with an even hypotenuse and those with an odd. For the former diagram we must invoke the theorem that if the hypotenuse is even, both legs of a numerical right triangle are also even; for the latter, that a difference of squared odd numbers is always a multiple of eight. (These theorems are easily demonstrated by means of dot-arithmetic.) The assumption in each case that the constructed side is commensurable with the unit side—that it has the ratio of a number to a number with the unit side—leads to the violation of an underlying principle: in the three-foot case that a number cannot be *both* even and odd; in the five-foot case that a number cannot be *neither* even nor odd.

But when we come to the case of the seventeen-foot square—which in this reconstruction does not constitute a separate paradigm, but is an example of the construction involving a triangle with an odd hypotenuse —the method appears to fail:

Because eight is manifestly a multiple of four, we cannot

prove, by means of the second of our paradigm proofs, that the root of the seventeen-foot square is incommensurable with the unit. This represents a distinct entanglement.

Theaetetus next says, in McDowell's translation,

ἡμῖν οὖν εἰςῆλθέ τι τοιοῦτον, ἐπειδὴ ἄπειροι τὸ πλῆθος αἱ δυνάμεις ἐφαίνοντο, πειραθῆναι συλλαβεῖν εἰς ἕν, ὅτῳ πάσας ταύτας προσαγορεύσομεν τὰς δυνάμεις.

Well, since the powers seemed to be unlimited in number, it occurred to us to do something on these lines: to try to collect the powers under one term by which we could refer to them all.

The οὖν in the first line, however, is most naturally taken as continuative, and not as some kind of ambiguous disjunctive. Here is a better translation of the above sentence, filled out to show how it follows on the peculiar problem brought on by the case of the seventeen-foot square:

Then [in our difficulty] something of this sort

occurred to us: since the squares [equal to odd numbers which have incommensurable sides] were appearing to be unlimited in multitude, to attempt to collect them under one term, by which we shall in future call all such squares [thereby distinguishing them from squares equal to odd numbers which *do* have commensurable sides].

It must be remembered that the seventeen-foot square foiled our technique by behaving like the square of an odd number (e.g., nine), a number with a rational root: the square on the even leg of its proof diagram was a multiple of eight. It is therefore natural that the idea for a new start, which occurs to Theaetetus in his perplexity over the breakdown of Theodorus' method, involves first distinguishing between those odd numbers with a rational and those with an irrational root (later classified as types, respectively, of square and oblong number).

Several kinds of interpretation of the passage must fall by the wayside. Theodorus' 'lesson' is not a pedagogical exercise, where the answers are already known and the cases selected for display. Nor is the episode included by Plato merely to make historical concessions (however vague or however specific) to the achievements of Theaetetus and his instructor. Theodorus' was a genuine investigation, which lighted on a genuine perplexity; Theaetetus' new definitions, which keyed his future researches, grew out of an attempt to resolve this perplexity.

We may now reconstruct Theaetetus' reasoning in full. Two aspects of Theodorus' technique break down in the seventeen-foot case. The first is the principle that underlies the preceding proofs, that a number must be either even or odd. In this case the principle leads to no absurdity; indeed, the proof presents no obstacle to the idea that the side of the seventeen-foot square is a normal odd number (!). The fundamental Pythagorean division among numbers by even and odd, which in a sense characterizes the ἀριθμός concept—the 'even and odd' is sometimes used as a synonym for ἀριθμός in Plato[12]— proves to be of limited utility in the study of incommensurable lengths. Theaetetus must look for a new fundamental characteristic of number in which to ground

---

[12] see e.g. *Laws* 818c, *Epinomis* 990c

the investigation of incommensurability. The second breakdown occurs in Theodorus' method of construction. Each of the odd numbers is figured as a square. This is possible because every odd number equals a difference of consecutive square numbers (in Pythagorean terms, the odd numbers are the series of gnomons which produce one square number from another). Our method for generating the odd squares, by constructing right triangles with pairs of consecutive integers (producing consecutive square numbers on the other leg and hypotenuse), works for this reason. But when all the odds are figured as squares, one cannot make out the perfect, rational-sided squares among them (like nine, twenty-five, etc.) from the rest. The method points this up by failing to distinguish between such perfect squares and cases like seventeen.

Theaetetus tackles both problems in one deft move. He makes a fresh division of all number (τὸν ἀριθμὸν πάντα, 147e) which will now isolate perfect squares from the rest, in place of the distinction by even and odd. If my interpretation is correct, an entanglement in a demonstration based on a geometrical representation of odd numbers by Theodorus has led to a geometrical distinction amongst *all* numbers by Theaetetus. The new name he was seeking for the odd squares whose sides are incommensurable is 'promecic', or oblong; which is to say, they are no longer thought of as squares at all. This category includes, of course, many even numbers as well, and the new generality is marked by Theaetetus: three and five and πᾶς ὃς ἀδύνατος ἴσος ἰσάκις γενέσθαι, 'every number which is unable to be generated as equal-times-equal', belongs to the new class (148a). The even-odd distinction belonged to number as such; the new one arises from a geometrical interpretation of number. But the whole problem of incommensurability arises in the interface between number and magnitude: hence the new definitions might be expected to suggest new solutions in this difficult domain.

Theaetetus for the first time exploits the breakdown of the geometrical analogy so that it becomes heuristic: whereas in geometry, every rectangle can be reduced to a square of equal size, whose length of side is the geometric mean in relation to the sides of the rectangle, a promecic *number* cannot be reduced to a square number. The side of the square which equals a promecic number becomes the new referent, in Theaetetus' scheme, for the word δύναμις (plural δυνάμεις); it is described by Theaetetus as incommensurable with a μῆκος (plural μήκη), his name for the side of a true square number. The geometrical analogy allows this δύναμις to be conceived of as the irrational geometric mean between the rational factors of an oblong number.

Theaetetus first describes the promecic number, in relation to the square number, as τὸν τοίνυν μεταξὺ τούτου, 'the number which is therefore in between this'. (147e) On the level of plane numbers, the inferential description makes sense; oblong numbers (2, 3, 5, 6, 7, etc.) are scattered in between the square numbers (4, 9, 16, etc.). On the level of the associated lines, however, this description becomes far more interesting. The δυνάμεις lie between the μήκη as geometric means that bring them into relation.

The unifying power of the mean proportional is one of its seminal virtues. Theaetetus' achievement is to conceive of the irrational roots for the first time as mean proportionals. This allows them to be seen no longer as perplexing and intractable, but as types of beings that in fact unite all number—no longer stumbling blocks to number theory, but the essential intermediaries that relate numbers to each other. To describe both the μῆκος and the δύναμις as sides of squares is to emphasize their nature as mean proportionals: a μῆκος is the rational geometric mean between the unit and a square number; the δύναμις is the irrational geometric mean between two μήκη, the rational factors of an oblong number.

What was once unutterable and unreckonable can now give an account of itself: a δύναμις, lying 'in between', is commensurable with a μῆκος *in square only*. So successful was this account that such a line, commensurable in square, is henceforward called ῥητός in the ancient world,[13] 'utterable', 'expressible', even 'rational' (although the modern convention reverts to

---

[13] see Euclid, *Elements* X Def. 3

calling its length 'irrational'). To be sure there are still irrational lines left—those that are commensurable neither in square nor in length—but Theaetetus' new definitions allow the roots of rational squares to be seen as not the opposite of what is rational or utterable (ἄ-λογα or ἄρ-ρητα), but merely as 'other', different in kind.

This classification of Theaetetus' may well be the specific paradigm for Plato's solution to the Parmenides problem (see *Sophist* 257b ff.). Not-being is not the opposite (ἐναντίον) of being, says the Eleatic stranger, but what is 'other' (ἕτερον) in relation to being; moreover, the nature of the other is proved to exist and 'to be chopped up in small bits distributed over all beings in their relations to one another' (κατακεκερματισμένην ἐπὶ πάντα τὰ ὄντα πρὸς ἄλληλα, 258d-e). Behind the metaphor lies a mathematical paradigm: Theaetetus has distributed the not-rational amongst all number (τὸν ἀριθμὸν πάντα), as the geometric means which define the relationships between numbers.

The notion of the heuristic paradigm takes on a central significance for Plato in the *Politicus*. It informs a new conception of philosophical inquiry.[14] One is to approach the unfamiliar and unknown by placing it alongside the known and the familiar, so that elements (στοιχεῖα) and combinations (συλλαβαί) in the latter become paradigmatic for possible ways of interpreting the former. The whole analysis of weaving in that dialogue is meant to serve as an instructive paradigm for the analysis of the statesman. Theaetetus' classifications demonstrate this method. By bringing alongside something familiar from geometry—the reducibility of rectangles to equal squares via the geometric mean—he is able to discern a new classification of all number, one which elegantly circumscribes the irrational.

The 'paradigmatic method' is to characterize his future researches as well. The commentator to Euclid's Book X (thought to be Pappus) implies that Theaetetus took the arithmetic, harmonic, and geometric means, all of them now considered rational, as models for three new, profoundly irrational lines, the binomial, apotome, and

---

[14]see *Politicus* 278b-e

medial.[15] At the end of Book X (Prop. 115), the last of these is then shown to define a further, infinite class of irrational lines. At each stage, the unfamiliar is made known by means of the familiar; the ἄρρητον is analysed and combined in terms of the elements and syllables of the ῥητόν. Its parts can then be classified and named, and the unutterable becomes more and more conversant. At *Theaetetus* 202B, Socrates describes a dream which teaches him that elements are ἄλογα, while combinations are ῥηταί. It is therefore fitting that Theaetetus' act of combination (συλλαβεῖν εἰς ἕν, 147e), based on a geometrical paradigm, renders its object ῥητόν, 'expressible'. The Eleatic stranger intends, at *Politicus* 278e, that this kind of inquiry by means of paradigms may bring us to a state of waking, instead of a dream (ὕπαρ ἀντ' ὀνείρατος).

---

[15]see Euclid, *The Elements*, 3 vols., Vol. 3, ed. Sir Thomas Heath, Annapolis: St. John's College Press, 1947, 3

B. *A Parmenidean Portent*

The peculiar nature of the irrational geometric mean between rational factors, Theaetetus' δύναμις, may well have served as the paradigmatic inspiration for Plato's new solutions to both the Parmenidean and the Protagorean paradoxes. This will become clearer as we examine the peculiar ontological and epistemological characteristics of this δύναμις.

With regard to its ontology, viewed from the geometrical standpoint, the irrational mean offers no intrinsic difficulties; it is a stable entity, a side of the square equal to a given rectangle, easily and elegantly constructible inside a circle.[16] But with regard to the way it comes to be known—the way it comes to be measured, from the arithmetical standpoint—it turns into a very shifty thing.

To measure a δύναμις, we have to make a promecic

---

[16]see Euclid II.14 and VI.13

number more and more square, so that its rational factors come to approximate the root. We do this by interpolating arithmetic and harmonic means between the two factors.[17] It can be shown (as by Proclus)[18] that for any two factors A and B, the harmonic mean C and the arithmetic mean D stand in this relation:

$$A : C :: D : B$$

This means that the rectangle AB equals the rectangle CD. Since AB is our oblong number, CD is an alternative representation of it. If one then interpolates two new means between C and D, and continues the process, one generates pairs of factors of the same number that become more and more equal, which give successively closer rational approximations to the geometric mean from above and below. Note that however many means one interpolates, the rational factors remain unequal, and

---

[17]Brown, '*Theaetetus*', 371 ff.

[18]Proclus, *In Platonis Timaeum Commentaria*, 3 vols., Vol. 2, ed. Ernst Diehl, Leipzig: Teubner, 1903-6, 173-4

oblong numbers never actually become squares. As Theaetetus describes an oblong number, 'a greater and a lesser side always contain it' (148a). Brown argues, following Toeplitz, that the use of 'always' (ἀεί) is significant here in its technical sense (i.e., that of Euclid's X.1 and X.2), and implies the application of a continued process.[19] (This 'technical' sense is in any case rooted in the everyday usage of this adverb, whose sense is both distributive with respect to instances of the subject, and frequentative with respect to the verb.) The text may be seen to allude to the continued process of interpolations described above, and to the fact that it can never yield equal sides for a rectangular number. The geometric mean stays in between: while A : X :: X : B, so also is C : X :: X : D, and C′ : X :: X : D′.

The interpolated means 'trap' the δύναμις length within an arbitrarily small interval. Each successive interpolation divides the previous interval between the rational factors by more than half: the new arithmetic mean cuts off exactly half from above, and the new

---

[19]Brown, '*Theaetetus*', 371

harmonic mean some more from below. By Euclid's X.1—a central theorem in applying the method of reciprocal measurement, ἀνθυφαίρεσις, which is associated with the mature Theaetetus—it follows that the interval between the successive pairs of arithmetic and harmonic means can be made to shrink smaller than any given magnitude. It is not only this interval that evanesces, but also the difference between the geometric mean and each of the other two means respectively. This means that the difference between the true length of the geometric mean and each of its under- and over-estimates is evanescent, and there is a strong inducement to see the irrational mean itself as characterized by the narrowing oscillation of its extremes.

This is not a naive interpretation of the measuring process: in the case of a rational geometric mean (Theaetetus' 'μῆκος') there is a number inside the interval which the estimates approach; but in the irrational case, there appears to be no normal numerical entity involved, and we do not know how exactly the mean behaves inside the decreasing rational interval which defines it. We only know that at each stage, it lies in between the harmonic and the arithmetic estimates, while approaching each of them in turn to less than any given difference.

There is evidence in the *Epinomis* that an irrational geometric mean was thought of as oscillating between the arithmetic and harmonic ones (see 991a-b). In a passage which extols the ubiquity and power of τὸ διπλάσιον, 'the double', in proportions, the Athenian stranger turns to the means associated with this interval. He gives standard definitions of the pair of rational means (amounting to the fact that the arithmetic is equidistant from its extremes, and the harmonic differs from its extremes by the same proportional part of each one); he then points out that in the interval between six and twelve, they are called the ἡμιόλιον and the ἐπίτριτον. He adds that in between these same ones (τούτων αὐτῶν ἐν τῷ μέσῳ) is a proportion that has been given to the dance of the Muses, 'which turns itself about toward both of them' (ἐπ' ἀμφότερα στρεφομένη).

We first observe that the ἀριθμός concept involved not just concrete assemblages, but also 'repetition' numbers (i.e., δίς, τρίς, etc.).[20] Therefore if we investigate any example of doubleness, or 'twice', we are just as specifically studying 'the two' as when in studying a particular isosceles triangle, we can prove things about all isosceles triangles *qua* isosceles. The interval 12:6 is an example of 2:1, of τὸ διπλάσιον διάστημα or the 'double interval'.[21] The practical advantage of studying higher multiples of a given interval is that the rational means can be interpolated without fractioning the unit. In the interval 12:6, the arithmetic and harmonic means are nine and eight respectively; hence the stranger describes their ratios with the lower extreme as the ἡμιόλιον (9:6 reduces to 3:2) and the ἐπίτριτον (because 8:6 reduces to 4:3). If we then interpret the object which turns itself about ἐπ' ἀμφότερα as the oscillating geometric mean between the two rational means, the other phrase describing it (τούτων αὐτῶν ἐν τῷ μέσῳ) becomes explicable; for we recall that this object is not only the geometric mean in

---

[20]see David H. Fowler, *The Mathematics of Plato's Academy*, Oxford: Clarendon Press, 1987, 14 ff.

[21]see Plato, *Timaeus* 36a for this usage

the interval 12:6, but also in the interval 9:8, defined by the pair of rational means (the referents of τούτων αὐτῶν) inside 12:6. Since the division between nine and eight happens also to represent a division in the seventeen steps of the epic hexameter, the dance of the Muses, the writer draws a connection between the dynamic geometric mean in the double interval and the turning point in the dance.[22]

At *Parmenides* 129b, a young Socrates asserts that 'if someone proved that similar things in themselves (αὐτὰ τὰ ὅμοια) became dissimilar (ἀνόμοια), or the dissimilar similar, that would, I think, be a portent (τέρας).' Theaetetus' δύναμις is the portent made manifest: insofar as it is the length of a square, the one which equals an oblong number, it is ὅμοιον; but insofar as it is approximated to the point of identity by unequal rational factors, it is forever ἀνόμοιον. ὁμοίωσις is the principle Theaetetus has applied to number; in the new arithmetic,

---

[22] for an extended discussion of the significance of this description for the form of the Homeric hexameter, see A. P. David, *The Dance of the Muses: Choral Theory and Ancient Greek Poetics*, Oxford: Oxford University Press, 2006, pp. 94-137, esp. 94-102

one makes 'unlike' (ἀνόμοιοι) promecic numbers more and more square, or 'like' (ὅμοιοι). The upshot is that arithmetic becomes conceived of as a kind of geometry, and indeed, by the time of the *Epinomis*, the entire activity of geometry itself is characterized as the 'making like' of *numbers* that are by nature unlike (*Epinomis* 990d). The Athenian stranger is led to describe this numerical geometry as a wonder, of divine and not human origin. Perhaps he is thinking about the δύναμις, the portent which it seeks to generate.

I earlier suggested that the relation of the δύναμις to all number stood in direct analogy with the nature of the 'other' to all being. This 'other' was the basis for Plato's new conception of not-being; he was concerned to show both that it exists and that it is distributed over all being in its inter-relationships (*Sophist* 258d-e). This second characteristic seems clearly to implicate the δύναμις as a paradigm; but does Plato ever try to demonstrate its existence? If this object, like and unlike, at rest and oscillating, is to be the object-paradigm which recasts all the hoary debates and turns them on their heads, he must have been at pains to show that it actually exists.

A key passage in the *Politicus* answers this expectation. The Eleatic stranger highlights its importance by referring explicitly to the pivotal argument in the *Sophist* about not-being: just as there the hunt for the sophist was saved by the argument that not-being exists,

> οὕτω καὶ νῦν τὸ πλέον αὖ καὶ ἔλαττον μετρητὰ προσαναγκαστέον γίγνεσθαι μὴ πρὸς ἄλληλα μόνον ἀλλὰ καὶ πρὸς τὴν τοῦ μετρίου γένεσιν; οὐ γὰρ δὴ δυνατόν γε οὔτε πολιτικὸν οὔτ' ἄλλον τινὰ τῶν περὶ τὰς πράξεις ἐπιστήμονα ἀμφισβητήτως γεγονέναι τούτου μὴ ξυνομολογηθέντος.   (*Politicus*, 284b-c)

so also now, are we not compelled to say that the greater and the less come to be measured not only against one another, but also toward the generation of the mean? For it is impossible at any rate, that either the statesman, or any one else who has knowledge about practical affairs, should indisputably come to exist, if this is not agreed on.

Politics, practical undertakings, and works of art direct

themselves to what is fitting (τὸ μέτριον). If such a thing cannot be proven to exist, the possibility of τέχνη itself comes into question. The stranger proposes a new division of the science of measurement (μετρητική, 283d). The first part involves measurement of greater against less; this would determine relative excess or deficiency, and, presumably, whether or not there was a common measure (by the technique of ἀνθυφαίρεσις). The second part involves measurement towards a mean separated from extremes (εἰς τὸ μέσον ἀπῳκίσθη τῶν ἐσχάτων, 284e); and it is likely that the geometric mean, the mean proportional, is especially meant. Since this mean is the one which squares the greater-by-less, bringing extremes into balance and making the ἀνόμοιον ὅμοιον, it must be the one whose preservation brings beauty to works of art (284a-b); the famous 'golden' mean is a species of geometric mean.

The method of interpolating pairs of rational means as greater and lesser approximations of the geometric mean admirably suits the terms of Plato's description:

μεῖζόν τε ἅμα καὶ ἔλαττον μετρεῖσθαι πρὸς ἄλληλα
μόνον, ἀλλὰ καὶ πρὸς τὴν τοῦ μετρίου γένεσιν.

(284d)

The greater-and-less are at the same time measured not only against each other, but also toward the generation of the fitting.

Note that 'greater-and-less' are paired off by τε-και, and that they are to be measured 'toward the generation' (γένεσις) of the mean. At each stage of the interpolations, one is not comparing the extremes with each other to find their common measure or their relative excess or deficiency, but one is manipulating the *pair* of extremes to generate a number in between them. Take the case of B less than A, for example; one does not subtract B from A to find their difference, but rather one adds the pair together and halves the result, generating the arithmetic mean (D). (In the case of the double, 12:6, we get D = (12 + 6)/2 = 18/2 = 9.) Then one multiplies the pair together and divides the result by the arithmetic mean, to produce the harmonic mean C. (C = (12 × 6)/D = 72/9 = 8.)

C and D then become the new pair of greater-and-less (D′
= (C + D)/2 = (9 + 8)/2 = 17/2 = 8 1/2; C′ = (C × D)/D′ = (9 ×
8)/(17/2) = 72/(17/2) = 144/17 = 8 8/17). Notice how the
product of each *pair* ({C, D}, {C′, D′}) remains the same (72)
and how quickly the interpolations converge (the
difference between C′ and D′ is already only 1/34th part of
the unit). The whole process is continually generating the
μέτριον, the geometric mean which runs in the middle of
them all (μεταξύ) and unites the series of pairs into one
(as it is put in *Theaetetus*, συλλαβεῖν εἰς ἕν).

But if the mean is never reached, can it be shown
to exist? The proof would appear to depend on the
ontological interdependence of the arts, the μέτριον, and
the pairs of greater-and-less. The stranger declares that
we must suppose both that the arts exist, and that the
greater-and-less are measured toward the generation of
the mean:

> τούτου τε γὰρ ὄντος ἐκεῖνα ἔστι, κἀκείνων οὐσῶν
> ἔστι καὶ ταῦτα[23], μὴ δὲ ὄντος ποτέρου τούτων

---

[23]The reading of B and T; editors usually read τοῦτο

οὐδέτερον αὐτῶν ἔσται ποτέ.   (284d)

For if this [the mean] exists, those [the greater-and-
less] exist, and if those arts exist, these [the greater-
and-less] also exist, but if one of them [the mean or
the arts] does not exist, neither of this pair [the
greater nor the less] ever will.

The passage is admittedly very difficult, in text and
translation, because of a possible ambiguity as to the
referents of the correlated demonstratives; but it seems
clear that an existence proof is at issue.

That the greater and the less exist, no one would
dispute. But if we deny the existence of either the μέτριον
or the arts, each by means of which the greater-and-less
are made known and defined, we run the risk of denying
the existence of this pair of fundamental opposites. Hence
we accept, provisionally at least (284d), the existence of
the mean. The greater-and-less measured against one
another discover a common measure or the unit—Plato's
paradigm, perhaps, for that which is. Measured toward
the generation of the mean, they discover a measure in
between the greater and the less, which still *is* greater-

and-less; a measure that is always coming to be, in the relations between things that are. In this relational mode of being, Plato has his paradigm for the 'other', and a beachhead against Parmenidean ontology.

C. *A Protagorean Paradox*

Plato's answer to the Protagorean conundrums on flux is also based on this new branch of μετρητική, measurement toward the γένεσις of the mean. At *Sophist* 247d-e, the stranger sets it down as a provisional solution to their paradoxes, that whatever possesses a power (δύναμις) to act or be acted upon, even only once, is truly existent, and then formally defines beings (τὰ ὄντα) as οὐκ ἄλλο τι πλὴν δύναμις, nothing else than δύναμις. It is highly unlikely that such a word could be both novelly and proximately applied by Plato without some sort of cross-reference.

This answer, that being is δύναμις, comes after the stranger has cornered these thinkers into admitting that the incorporeal exists in some way. The 'flux theorists' have then to say what being is, in a way that covers both the corporeal and the incorporeal (247d). I must therefore show how Theaetetus' δύναμις is a saving answer on both these levels. Let us return to the *Theaetetus*, where a Protagorean theory of sensation based on mutual measurement gets a thorough setting out by Socrates, and where once again the non-corporeal is required to exist.

Brown has led the way, by showing that Socrates' version of the Protagorean theory of sensation is modeled on the continued process of interpolation to approximate the geometric mean.[24] The odd expressions in this passage of text become happily explicable on these terms. Here are some of Brown's list of correlations: 'the object sought is ... an "in-between" (μεταξύ τι) (154a), which ... is to be identified by a process of "measuring and being measured" (παραμετρούμεθα ... παραμετρούμενον) (154b)'; 'the object determined "is nothing in itself, but is becoming for someone always" (οὐδὲν εἶναι ἓν αὐτὸ καθ' αὑτό, ἀλλά τινι ἀεὶ γίγνεσθαι) (157a-b; cf. 153e)'; and 'the intermediate stages of the process are "infinite in number, but paired off" (πλήθει μὲν ἄπειρα, δίδυμα δέ) (156a-b).' In this last passage we can add some very telling details: it is out of the coming together and rubbing against one

---

[24]Brown, 'Theaetetus', 376-7

another (ὁμιλίας τε καὶ τρίψεως πρὸς ἄλληλα) of that which has the power (δύναμις) to act, and that which has the power to undergo, that the infinite, twinned offspring come; these paired offspring, the sensed thing and the sensation of it, are 'forever falling out together and being generated' (ἀεὶ συνεκπίπτουσα καὶ γεννωμένη). For ἀεὶ συνεκπίπτουσα, we could as well have rendered: 'being interpolated together, in a continued process'. The notion that an object of sense and a sensation are mutually measured, and that they are infinite, paired-off interpolations, can hardly belong to any 'common sense' theory of sensation; Brown can produce a concrete, mathematical analogy which could have motivated this otherwise bizarre formulation.

The key to this analogy is that Socrates' Protagoreans explain the phenomenon of sensation as one of mutual measurement of object and percipient. This way of thinking, by the old version of μετρητική, leads to their positions on the ultimate relativity of experience; measurement πρὸς ἄλληλα generates a common measure or unit, but since each percipient and the entire world of sense are in constant flux, and their interaction with one another changes them both, this unit is redefined by each sense event. Unity in sense-experience is therefore dependent on the particular state of a human being at a particular time; man is the measure of all things.

Plato's solution is to apply the new theory of measurement: he accepts the premise of mutual measurement in sensation, but he can now generate a kind of unity that is independent of subject and object, at the same time that it embraces them. To call the opposed poles of measurement δυνάμεις (156a) is to signal their relation, not to each other, but as first approximations of the mean proportional which defines and unites them both. One has not done away with flux by any means; Socrates ill and Socrates healthy each define different 'intervals' with the same wine, so that the series of interpolated means are also different (yielding the sensation of sweetness in one case and bitterness in the other, 159c-e). But one has analysed sense phenomena in a way that reveals unique classes within them; the geometric means define infinite series of correlated sense experiences.

The point of defining being as δύναμις, the capacity to act or to be acted upon, even only once, is to show that even the most random and isolated phenomenon, occurring once to a single percipient, in and of itself defines an infinite class through the mean it generates. The upshot is, as Brown observes, that 'the flux of phenomena may after all be "saved" for knowledge.'[25] The ingenuity of the approach is that the very fact which made such experience seem intractable for science, that the 'rubbing' of perceived object against percipient observer changes them both, is now made the essential condition for generating unity in phenomena (represented by the geometric mean) via a continued process. This is the same ingenuity that Theaetetus displayed when he solved the problem of incommensurability by newly exploiting the relation between geometrical figures and numbers, which had created the trouble in the first place.

The need to admit the existence of the incorporeal

---

[25]Ibid., 377

is demonstrated by the need for some faculty within us to account for our ability to compare data, to recognize what is common to all and to categorize experience in terms of the philosophical oppositions (i.e., being and not-being, like and unlike, etc.).[26] Theaetetus is convinced that this is done by the soul, and cannot be done by any one of the bodily sense organs; for which he is called 'beautiful' (καλός) by Socrates (185d-e). If this faculty can compare sense data from different organs, then its work consists in comparing means, which are expressed as ratios in terms of their respective extremes (like the ἡμιόλιον and ἐπίτριτον in the *Epinomis* passage, 991b). Therefore this faculty compares ratios, and its activity must be the calculation of proportions (ἀναλογίζειν). As strained as this might sound, Socrates' choice of words bears out the analogy: the word used to describe this faculty's ability is συλλογισμός ('calculation', 186d); the verb which characterizes its activity is ἀναλογίζομαι (186a), and the products of its work are ἀναλογίσματα ('proportions', 186c). The theory of sensation had entailed

---

[26]see *Theaetetus* 185c

that the objects of sense be commensurable with their proper sense organ (ξύμμετρον, 156d). But one cannot hear through sight or see through hearing (184e-185a). Therefore the faculty which has to compare and to 'square' the data from *different* sense organs, must deal with problems of incommensurability. We have already seen how Theaetetus' δύναμις has helped to facilitate such studies.

The answer that being is δύναμις is therefore shown to resolve both the corporeal and incorporeal aspects of flux theory as Socrates presents them—in such a way as to gather them into one account—if an explicit reference is taken to Theaetetus' δύναμις, and the new branch of measurement science. Sense phenomena can then be shown to have a ratio (ἔχειν λόγον), because object and sense organ generate a mean, and the percipient soul becomes a kind of λογιστικός or μετρητικός ('ratio-' or 'measure-calculator'), because the new techniques allow for the handling of incommensurability.

Clearly, the aims of Plato's application of

measurement theory to sense perception are not the same as those of modern science. No actual measurements are generated, for example. (The whole thing turns a bit silly if numbers are plugged in.) Plato's aim might rather have been, in the spirit of ancient astronomy, to 'save the appearances'. As I understand this notion, it does not mean 'to reduce the appearances to measurement'. To save the appearances is, in Brown's phrase, to 'save' phenomena for knowledge, by supplying a rational construct in the form of a mathematical model that could account for, or at least correspond to, the perceived data. This is the kernel of a paradigmatic method. There is no necessary entailment of a claim that the model has a causal relationship to the appearances, or that it represents the physical reality standing 'behind' the appearances; it has rather the free, associative illumination of a paradigm. This was true even for Ptolemaic astronomy, where the principle of uniform circular motion did eventually generate accurately predictive models for the perceived non-uniform orbits in the heavens. This achievement in astronomy of predictive correspondence between hypotheses and phenomena set a standard thereafter for the saving of appearances. In Plato's time, however, Eudoxus devised astronomical models that could not have been accurately predictive; yet they could still have been seen to 'save' the appearances, in that such salvation might have been seen to come through the ascent itself, from the spangled particularity of sensual observation to the realm of the mathematical. Rather than recording the movements of the decorations on the celestial ceiling, which one perceives by sight—see Plato's disparaging remarks on the current state of astronomy (*Republic* 529a ff.)—Eudoxus was developing models for them, based on the mathematics of uniform circular motion, which one grasps by argument and reason. To reduce the disorder and particularity of appearances in the sensible world to mathematical generality and principled order would be to *save* the appearances—*for* reason, and *from* chaos. The reduction requires at least a qualitative correspondence between paradigm and reality; hence Eudoxus' models had to be able to reproduce retrogressions in the orbits of the outer planets. It took a considerable refinement in the models and the observations—and possibly in philosophical outlook as well—to achieve the quantitative correspondence in Hipparchus and Ptolemy, where the retrograde motions were given by the models in magnitude and in time. Even Ptolemy, however, is concerned to distinguish his work and discipline as *mathematics*, and not physics or theology, although it makes some concessions to these other fields. To the mathematician, in contrast with the physicist or theologian, the existence of different, equivalent models, such as eccentric circles and epicycles, or even heliocentricity and geocentricity, is a point of contemplative delight; for those others, a point of anxiety and dispute.

When it comes to the sublunary sphere, Plato accepts the premise of radical flux. He apparently held this view all his intellectual life (see Aristotle's biography, *Metaphysics* 987a30 ff.). All things are in motion, and so are their measures (i.e., the individual percipients); hence the measurements they take—individual perceptual judgements of things as to their sensible quality or size—are also in flux. (The same wind can appear hot and cold to different people, 152b.) The premise of flux apparently entails the premise, 'nothing is one in itself' (152d); this is the mathematical version of the relativist premise, 'there is no objective measure'. Different percipients—and the same percipient at different times—represent different measures, and hence there exists a problem of radical incommensurability between individual perceptions. There can therefore be no question of a quantitative application of measurement theory to the phenomena. The very fact that perceptual events and judgements are judged to be completely unique and individual (ἴδιον—see, e.g., 154a) should suggest that they are not susceptible to general treatment of any kind, let alone to mathematical treatment. The world of sense, when approached in terms of these kinds of premises, ought not to be salvageable for knowledge.

All the same, for the metaphor of sensation as measurement, a notion attributed in the *Theaetetus* ultimately to Protagoras (152a), there is life yet. The new branch of measurement science can supply an intriguing model for at least a qualitative saving of the appearances. Here, as in the sublunary sphere, we also have things and their measures, extremes and means, continually changing. But this does not prevent them from being related to a single magnitude—to two definite magnitudes, in fact, for the size of the rectangle contained by each pair of interpolations, as well as its geometric root, remains the same. Hence there *can* be a kind of unity predicated of a continued process of change; and so perhaps a predication of unity need not be precluded from sense experience, even in a world of unceasing flux. In addition, the measure of the root of this constant magnitude represented by the rectangles, the geometric mean approximated by the arithmetic and harmonic means, is a measure that is continually *coming to be*, but never *is*. As such, it is uniquely suited as a qualitative model or paradigm for perception, which seems to share this property in the sensible world. That which is (τὰ ὄντα) *comes to be*, as a perception, through a continued process of measurement with the percipient. The first step in applying the new kind of measurement as a theory of perception would be to say, with the Eleatic stranger, that being (τὰ ὄντα) is δύναμις.

D. *Paradigmatic Dice*

The vastly different implications of the two kinds of measurement are brought out by Socrates' example of the dice (154c). If one compares six dice with four dice they look greater, but if one compares six dice with twelve, they look less. This seems to involve a paradox, because nothing can ever become greater or less in size or number while it remains equal to itself. Two other postulates are said to contend with this one and with each other in our souls, when we think about the six dice becoming greater and less: anything in respect of which nothing is added or subtracted is neither increased nor diminished, but is always equal; and that which did not exist before could not exist afterwards without a process of becoming (154a-b).

Brown has pointed out that the way Socrates compares six with four and twelve—that the difference in each case is half of the compared term (154c)—is an explicit recognition of six as the harmonic mean in the interval defined by four and twelve as extremes.[27] He then takes the reference to the harmonic mean as an allusion to the geometric mean in the interval, to which the three postulates mentioned above apply in a mathematically interesting way—a way that justifies Theaetetus' dizziness at such paradoxes (155c). This is by way of defending Plato against the likes of Bertrand Russell, who refers to Plato's difficulties in these matters as 'among the infantile diseases of philosophy.'[28] The text does not support Brown's defence, however. Socrates and Theaetetus seem genuinely perplexed by any three-term comparison, whether among dice or between the size of Socrates and two stages of a growing Theaetetus (155b-c). This is because the art of measurement (but not necessarily philosophy) is in its infancy; mutual measurement (πρὸς ἄλληλα) can only distinguish the greater and the less, and the intermediate objects inevitably called up by a three-term comparison become equivocal in a rather

---

[27]Brown, '*Theaetetus*', 374

[28]quoted in Brown, '*Theaetetus*', 373, note 38

straightforward way. The concreteness of the cited examples—remember that Plato always talks about dice—may help to reinforce the odd intuition that an object changes into its opposite while staying the same.

The new branch of μετρητική, measurement toward the generation of the mean, legitimizes the intermediate. It generates objects that are definitively 'in between' all rational numbers, as we have seen. (This radical in-betweenness of the non-rational square root is reflected in Dedekind's 'cut'.) Plato's presentation points the way to the mature science of measurement. Comparing six dice to four and twelve is to measure tangible quantities against one another, so as to cause perplexity about the relativity of six; seeing 6 as the harmonic mean in the interval 12:4 is to see it as a generating approximation of the only non-relative, or 'trans-relative', entity inside that interval: the geometric mean or mean proportional. As one generates it geometrically, it exists unchanged and remains equal with itself. As one generates it arithmetically, it is now greater now less, now increased and now diminished, continually coming to be. The geometric mean is therefore an exception to each of the three Protagorean assumptions about relativity, just as it was to the Parmenidean ones about sameness and being; and we have already seen how Plato tries to prove that it exists.

Brown was right, therefore, in recognizing the reference to the harmonic mean and its allusion to the geometric mean, but he was at least partly wrong about the significance of the allusion. That the same number or magnitude can be called both greater and less seems to be regarded as a genuine paradox; the problem can be nullified by re-thinking the process of measurement, as a generation of means, rather than as a direct comparison of quantities. A mean *is* a mean in relation to what is greater and to what is less; the greater and the less, in turn, are so in relation, as extremes to a mean. Hence extremes and means can only exist and be defined in terms of each other. A mean is therefore a thing that demands to be comprehended on *all* these terms: it is one thing remaining the same as itself, *and* it is greater, *and* it is less. The concatenation of these properties is no longer paradoxical, but rather uniquely definitive, in the case of a mean. The trick is therefore to define numbers and magnitudes, where the purported paradox of relativity is observed, as means.

This is precisely what Theaetetus has already done. Not just the incommensurable roots (δυνάμεις), but all numbers and commensurable lengths (μήκη) are re-cast as geometric means between the unit and square and oblong numbers (that is, as sides of the square representations of all numbers). This is once again to resolve a difficulty by re-defining its terms, and to resolve a paradox by exploiting its own conditions. Theaetetus can cure his dizziness by turning the *problem* upside down. To re-classify rational and irrational lengths as types of means is to make these relativistic creatures, with their seemingly paradoxical mixture of properties, the very standards of measurement; the 'in-between' now takes on the substantive existence in measurement science which once belonged exclusively to number. By referring to the problematical, 'in-between' six in such a way as to identify it as the harmonic mean in an interval, Plato would seem to be hinting at this kind of a solution during Socrates' very articulation of the paradox.

I do not mean to suggest, here or elsewhere, that the algorithm of interpolating means is some kind of cryptic code to Plato's meaning. For one thing, a mathematical model needs to be interpreted before it can be allegorized; in itself, the means algorithm is about measurement in the abstract and nothing else. (Even here, however, as I have suggested, the question 'what is a mean?' and the follow-up 'does it exist?' can have serious philosophical consequences, such as the postulating of a relational mode of being.) What I do see is the persistent heuristic and often playful application of a paradigm. The most serious and striking interpretation of this paradigm is as a theory of sense perception; but there are other exemplars in the *Theaetetus*. At 180e, Socrates tells Theodorus that by advancing little by little (κατὰ σμικρόν), they have unknowingly fallen into the midway position between the Parmenideans and the Heracliteans (εἰς τὸ μέσον πεπτωκότες—recall ἀεὶ συνεκπίπτουσα, 156b); their plight is compared to that of the people caught in the middle of a wrestling school tug-of-war, who are dragged toward opposite sides of the dividing line. On the one hand, this image is amusing and self-explanatory, and fully realized on its own terms. But one can discern behind it the notions, entirely neutral in themselves, of incremental interpolation toward the measurement of a mean, and oscillation around the measuring line. The mathematical model can hardly be said to explain or to interpret the image. The reverse is in fact the case: it is the tug-of-war which interprets, and gives content to, the paradigm. But just as in the case of Socrates' dice, an awareness of the underlying paradigm can suggest lines of thought that are textually based, and yet not necessarily part of the literal intention of the interlocutors in the dialogue. A mean is something which brings into relation and, in this sense, unites its extremes. It is therefore of considerable interest for a student of Socrates and Plato to wonder what a mean position between the Parmenideans and the Heracliteans might be like. The means algorithm and the image of the tug-of-war can be seen to do a double duty: conceiving of opposed positions no longer as opposites but as extremes is the first step towards our some day, as we still say, 'squaring' them, generating a solution in the mean between them; while at the same time, the image of being caught in the middle and pulled to either side captures the present predicament of the participants in the dialogue.

A significant portion of the *Theaetetus* is devoted to an exhaustive, case by case analysis of the possibility of false judgement, depending on the premise that with regard to each thing one might have an opinion about, one either knows it or one doesn't. But Theaetetus is forced to adopt this premise of polar, opposite conditions when Socrates asks him to leave out the states that lie in between knowledge and ignorance (μεταξὺ τούτων, 188a), such as learning and forgetting. I think few readers would agree with Socrates' claim here that these intermediate processes have no bearing on the discussion. Does not the text rather invite the reader to consider, on his own at any rate, the nature and the implications of such mean states as learning and forgetting? Are they not significant in themselves, and especially crucial as a basis for the task at hand, an investigation of the cognitive mechanism which might result in false opinion? The midway cases of learning and forgetting exhibit the paradoxes we have come to expect of means: it would seem that in the midst of these conditions, knowledge and ignorance are both present in the mind at the same time and about the same thing.

In the middle of the dialogue (172c-177b), Socrates digresses to paint the portraits of two incompatible human types, the man of the city and the philosopher. The opposite qualities of these figures take on a new significance if the figures are interpreted not as opposites, but as extremes. The reader will notice that the philosopher described is not in fact like Socrates: he is rather a latter-day Thales (173e ff.), an astronomer, physicist, geometer, and general investigator into the abstract natures of things; a man more reminiscent of Aristophanes' parody than Plato's Socrates. In the Socrates of the *Theaetetus* we see instead a mean between extremes, between the man of the law courts, whose time and speech are strictly circumscribed, and the philosopher, whose time and speech are all his own (172d-e). Socrates has the leisure, on the one hand, to pursue an investigation into the definition of knowledge with Theaetetus, including time for fresh starts and digressions (172d); on the other, we are reminded quite pointedly, by way of ending the conversation and the text, that Socrates has to break off until the next day so that he can keep his appointment in court, to meet Meletus' indictment. Socrates' time is not his own; and his life will depend upon his ability to speak the speech of the law courts.

It is tempting to compare Socrates' two patterns, his 'paradigms set up in the midst of existence' (176e), with the paradigms of Theaetetus. The divine and the perfectly just would be figured as four-square and ὅμοιον, and the human and the political as inherently heteromecic. A tragic dimension emerges if one interprets Socrates' models as themselves an investiture of the models of the measurement paradigm. We are encouraged to become more and more like the divine and the just; but it is a structural feature of the interpolation algorithm that however equal it becomes, the rectangle can never become square. The flight from our mortal nature toward the divine is described by Socrates as an ὁμοίωσις or assimilation to god; ὁμοίωσις itself (Socrates repeats the word, 176b) is then explained as becoming δίκαιον ('just') and ὅσιον ('holy') in the company of φρόνησις ('intelligence'). But in the mathematical setting, the process of ὁμοίωσις ('making like' or squaring) can never be completed; and the suggestion in this context may be that ultimately the divine is irreconcilable with the human, that the life of pure philosophy is finally incommensurable with the life of the city. The demands of the philosopher, who asks 'what is man?' (174b), can never completely escape the demands of society, and its conventional expectations of man. The life and death of Socrates embody a paradigmatic dilemma: however long and full the measure of his days, and hence however long the process, through the purgations of philosophy, of assimilation to the divine, of becoming truly just and holy and wise,—there will come a day of reckoning by a different number, and the city will lay its claim to him.

A further note about the dice: the interval 12:4 is a

species of the τριπλάσιον διάστημα, 3:1. The interpolated means, beginning with eight and six, are therefore fourth-multiple approximations of the side of the three-foot square. The full significance of the example is now manifest: it illustrates the new way to investigate incommensurable lengths, taking up again the first of Theodorus' cases, and applying the continued processes involved in the squaring of Theaetetus' oblong numbers.

E. *Dialectic Training via* Reductio *and* Exhaustion

In addition to that portentous entity, the δύναμις, two methods associated with my interpretation of the geometry lesson, proof by *reductio ad absurdum* and the method of exhaustion, also become paradigmatic for Plato in this trio of dialogues. The former may have long since been the inspiration for Socrates' familiar technique of reducing his interlocutor to perplexity. It shows up at various stages of the argument in the *Theaetetus*, as for example at 154c-d, where Theaetetus is reduced to both affirming and denying one of the Protagorean postulates we have just discussed. Whereas in mathematics, this method achieves the positive result of refuting a hypothesis, and proving its contrary, Plato romanticizes the notion somewhat for philosophy; he is interested in perplexity itself as a heuristic state, and marks the wonderment that it brings on in Theaetetus as a sign of his being a philosopher (155c-d). But Plato also relies on the rigorous conception of the proof: at a crucial point in the *Sophist*, it is proved that some of the forms and genera must mix with each other and others not, only because the other two possibilities, that none of them do or all of them do, have been reduced to absurdity (252e). The upshot is an unexpected discovery of the philosopher and his science, while Theaetetus and the stranger had been looking for the sophist (253c). Dialectic is the science which divides things by form (εἶδος) and genus (γένος), and he who is capable of this science is the one who can best discern the complex inter-relationships among the forms—which ones unite others, which are parts, which wholes, and which stand apart from mixing (253d-e).

The method of division, which characterizes the investigations into the sophist and the statesman and which is identified with dialectic (253d-e), is based on the method of exhaustion. This is the post-classical name for the continued process of measurement we are now familiar with. One 'exhausts' a magnitude by continually cutting off rational segments of it, each of them more than half of what is left. If these rational 'shavings' are strung together, one can approximate a length to an arbitrarily high degree of accuracy. Once again, as Plato invests the mathematical paradigm with the dress of the dialectical process, he romanticizes it: at *Sophist* 261a-b, Theaetetus complains that as they get closer to their quarry, the sophist keeps throwing 'problems' in their way, like successive defensive walls (προβλήματα); the stranger assures him that any attacker who can make 'continuous progress forward' (εἰς τὸ πρόσθεν ἀεὶ προιέναι) should be confident of success. And to be sure, while the stranger never fails to string together the divisions which 'measure' his subject (e.g., at 268c-d for the sophist), his main concern is at least equally with the division process itself, and with the training it provides in distinguishing classes (see *Politicus* 285c-d). But there is still a concession here to the mathematical: at *Politicus* 287c, the stranger advises that in these procedures, one must divide by a number as close as possible to two. This serves a double purpose; it maximizes the number of divisions that will need to be made, thereby increasing a student's experience with the handling of kinds, while also providing the minimum subtraction required (more than half),[29] to guarantee the 'exhaustion' of the subject.

The aim of the division process is still to produce a definition, and in this sense it can be see as a refinement on the original Socratic methodology. But definition is here seen, perhaps for the first time explicitly, as a kind of measurement; this is a return to the root meaning of the term, which involves the setting of limits or boundary marks (ὁρίζειν). The Forms only enter the picture as the necessary terms of division, and the measures generated, to 'trap' the undefined object in an exhaustive process. It would seem that a considerable point of departure for this new vision of dialectic lies in the notion of *forms as measures*.

That the philosopher and the philosopher's art can be characterized by these continued processes marks a stunning change in Plato's thought. Brown draws the following conclusion:

---

[29]Euclid, *Elements* X.1

... in *Theaetetus*, and apparently in response to a lively sense of the mathematical achievements of this companion and colleague, Plato seems to be yielding somewhat to an epistemological suggestion derived from Theaetetus' notion of continued processes. This would involve thinking that opinion, and perhaps even perception, if they can be processed in just the right way, ought to be taken seriously. Further, it would involve his thinking that knowledge is not fully characterized by the fixed and finished objects (Ideas) toward which it may proceed, but that it is at least partly characterized by the approximating process itself. This would mean that at least in one aspect of it, knowledge is a continued process of learning.[30]

I would make a stronger claim for Plato's development: the more usual theory of forms, which involved forms as paradigms in the sense of ideals, has been reformed or even replaced in these dialogues, on the inspiration of the new measurement paradigms created by Theaetetus. That Plato himself recognized a development is evidenced by his curious wording at *Sophist* 248a: he there refers to

---

[30]Brown, '*Theaetetus*', 379

certain idealists, who do not believe in motion and mixing, as 'the friends of the forms' (τοὺς τῶν εἰδῶν φίλους). That Plato could use such a phrase, in relation to what is usually thought of as his singular philosophical calling card, must have implications for those who would chart the history of his thought. Did these friends of the forms use to be friends of his? Or were they the older gentlemen described somewhat unflatteringly at 251c, possibly older, rival Socratics? If so, was the original theory of forms perhaps a Socratic or a Parmenidean invention?

However these questions are answered, and whatever is the true measure of the distance between Plato and the 'friends of the forms', the sum total of my arguments is that there a revolution in Plato's conception of epistemology and ontology, necessitated by the existence of the curious object at the heart of the new measurement science: the irrational geometric mean between rational factors, Theaetetus' δύναμις. This object and this science served as paradigms for a brave new approach to some very old and perplexing problems.

Perhaps there are grounds for a revolution in our sense of Plato's development, to match the turn in the man.

Chapter 2

The Mathematical Meaning of the 'Indeterminate Dyad'

I shall argue that the controversial developments—some would say the reversals—in Plato's later metaphysical outlook were in fact an inspired response to some truly epochal developments in the mathematics of his day; in particular, to certain seminal advances in the theory of the irrational. Following on my reading of the geometry lesson at *Theaetetus* 147, and of its significance for that dialogue and for the *Sophist* and the *Politicus*, I can now shed light on one of the most obscure notions associated with Plato, a thing known to Aristotle as the 'indeterminate dyad'. The discovery and description of this remarkable object—remarkable, all right, yet thoroughly non-mystical and mathematically legitimate—can be seen as the motive force behind some of the arguments and constructs in the late dialogue *Philebus*. In interpreting the ancient testimony, my reconstruction demonstrates that the mathematical meaning of the late Platonic metaphysics was either not transmitted to, or simply lost on, the successors of Plato and their critic Aristotle. But where the philosophers strayed, the mathematicians found a fruitful path: the conclusion to the work started by Theaetetus and Plato finds a home of concision and elegance in the mathematics of Euclid's Book X. A historian of ancient philosophy may have to distinguish in future between the academics who inherited Plato's arguments, and the mathematicians who understood them.

Evidence for a revision in Plato's thought, radical or not, comes from Aristotle's intellectual biography in *Metaphysics* A. He there refers to a καὶ ὕστερον, an 'even afterwards' in Plato's career (987b1). The passage is explicit that there was a before and an after in Plato's thinking which was not apparently defined by the death of Socrates. What is more, the change was apparently of some considerable moment; the whole force of the expression is in the καί; Plato is said to have accepted the premise of universal flux espoused by Cratylus and the Heracliteans, *even* afterwards. The theory of sensation we have discussed in the *Theaetetus* is an example of his new approach to an old premise, an approach based on a new mathematics of measurement.

A. *The Dyadic Series*

At one time during the geometry lesson in the *Meno*, Socrates counsels the slave boy, who is trying to find the line from which a square the double of a given square is generated, 'if you do not care to count it out, just point out what line it comes from' (εἰ μὴ βούλει ἀριθμεῖν, ἀλλὰ δεῖξον ἀπὸ ποίας, 84a). This is the vintage Socratic irony, a playful but possibly sinister half-telling: there is in fact no straightforward way to count out such a line with the same unit measures that count off the side of the given square. In a passage that means to inspire confidence in our ability to learn, Socrates hints at a shadowy impediment that lurks, even as the slave boy triumphs. This problem of incommensurability was the bane of measurement science—μετρητική, that science which assigns number to continuous magnitude—perhaps onwards from the time of Pythagoras. Measurement πρὸς ἄλληλα, mutual measurement, the reciprocal subtraction (ἀνθυφαίρεσις) of two magnitudes, came to an end or limit (πέρας) at the common measure of these magnitudes; but if the magnitudes were incommensurable, the process of subtracting the less from the greater, and then the remainder from the less, would continue indefinitely (i.e., it was unlimited, ἄπειρον). Such everyday magnitudes as the diagonals of squares with countable sides were ἄρρητον, inexpressible, or ἄλογον, irrational, in terms of those sides, an embarrassment to any serious measurement science.

The in-betweenness of irrational lengths with respect to rational (countable) ones—in the *Meno*, Socrates takes pains to show by a narrowing process that the required length, the side of an eight-foot square, lies somewhere in between two and three feet (83c-e)—may have been the clue to a new approach, the new branch of measurement science proposed by Plato's Stranger in the *Politicus* (283d ff.). Alongside measurement πρὸς ἄλληλα, there is now to be measurement πρὸς τὴν τοῦ μετρίου γένεσιν, measurement toward the generation of the mean. I have suggested that Theaetetus' seemingly humble

classification of roots (*Theaetetus* 147c ff.) was the ultimate
inspiration for this formulation; his novel use of the mean
proportional allows both number and magnitude (the
phenomena of arithmetic and geometry) to be subsumed
successfully under a revitalized and heuristic
measurement science.

'"Squaring" is the finding of the mean' (ὁ
τετραγωνισμὸς μέσης εὕρεσις, *De Anima* 413a20), and he
who defines it this way, says Aristotle, is showing the
cause of the fact in his definition. To square a given
rectangle, one has to find the mean proportional between
the lengths of its sides. Theaetetus distinguishes between
two kinds of length as sides of squares. Taken by itself, this
classification is hardly more than a new way of naming
the phenomena of measurement science. Even at this
stage, however, the roots of non-square numbers,
formerly irrational and intractable, have become more
expressible (ῥητά); they are at least commensurable in
square. A third category can now be envisioned—
incommensurability in length *and* in square—so that
where we had a polar division of opposites (rational-

irrational), now we have an enumeration of the phenomena: rational, expressible, irrational.

But the true mathematical utility of this re-classification lies in the lucid quality of the geometric mean. We recall that for any interval, this mean can be approximated in length by interpolating successive pairs of arithmetic and harmonic means within the given extremes. Since in a rational interval, like that between the unit and a non-square number, the interpolated means are also rational, and since they define an evanescent sequence of rational intervals around the same geometric mean, the incommensurable roots of non-square numbers can now be systematically approximated with numbers of their own. Each of these lengths, which we nowadays call $\sqrt{2}$, $\sqrt{3}$, $\sqrt{5}$, etc., is approximated as a geometric mean by one or more series, each unique and infinite, of arithmetic and harmonic means, which give better and better rational over- and under-estimates (respectively) of each incommensurable length. The process is unlimited in its degree of accuracy.

The uniqueness of each of these 'dyadic series',

corresponding to each of the incommensurable roots, is the key to their achievement. Numbers may now be introduced, in a mathematically useful and rigorous way, to describe the lengths of these roots. Measurement science can thereby fulfill its mission, once paralyzed in these cases, to *number* the greater and the less. Irrational roots are no longer vaguely 'in between': each dyad of interpolated means defines *all* rational lengths, whole or fractional, than which a particular incommensurable root is greater, and all than which it is less. Since the 'dyadic interval' can be made to shrink indefinitely, these incommensurable lengths have been uniquely measured in terms of a given unit, as uniquely as any commensurable length.

A rational length is measured by one number, a 'one many', a single collection of so- and so-many units (and fractional parts). These lengths are therefore measured both absolutely and relatively in terms of the unit length; one can answer the question, 'how many is it?' with respect to them. An irrational but expressible length, on the other hand, is measured by a series of pairs of numbers, a unique but 'unlimited' or 'indeterminate' dyad (ἀόριστος δύας). Such lengths are only relatively measured in terms of the unit; for them, one cannot answer the question 'how many is it?' with a definite number, but one can *always* answer the question, 'is it greater or less than this many?' There are now two ways in which number can be applied to continuous magnitude —with a normal ἀριθμός measured by the unit, or an indeterminate dyad of such ἀριθμοί—so that both the diagonal and the side of a square can be 'counted off' in terms of the *same unit length*.

The original significance of the unit and the indeterminate dyad can now be recognized in the context of the new branch of measurement science: the former is a measure of all *rational* means (including the roots of square numbers); the latter is a way of measuring all the *expressible* geometric means (the roots of rectangular numbers). It is a principle and product unique to the new branch, measurement toward the generation of the mean, for paired interpolation represents a way to 'generate' an expressible geometric mean numerically, and the resulting indeterminate dyad of greater and lesser values is a precise and exhaustive way to locate an expressible length within the scale of the rational continuum. (The distinction is mirrored, or perhaps obscured, in the fact that the two kinds of modern 'Real' number both constitute a Dedekind 'cut' in the number line.) The unit and the indeterminate dyad, the respective measures of rational and expressible means, are therefore rightly conceived as the two proper principles of that science which approaches measurement through the construction of means.

B. *An Enumerative Theory of Forms: the* Philebus

In the *Philebus* (23c ff.), Socrates proposes a four-part division of all beings. The first two segments cover the limited and the unlimited, the once all-embracing Pythagorean pair of opposites. The third division encompasses those beings produced by the mixture of the polar principles; this mixed category represents the distinctive late Platonic innovation in ontological thinking, outlined also in the *Sophist* (see 252e). A fourth division is enumerated to cover the cause of the mixing in the category of mixed beings.

At first glance, the mathematical subtext of this classification seems fairly straightforward. The unlimited stands for continuous magnitude, that which admits of being greater or less (24e); the limited stands for number and measure (25a-b). The mixed class stands, as could be expected, for continuous phenomena that admit of measurement or a scale: Socrates mentions music, weather, the seasons, and 'all beautiful things' (ὅσα καλὰ πάντα, 26a-b). The demiurge of the *Timaeus*, who constructs a cosmic musical scale out of elements he has mixed (35b ff.), could be seen as a mythical archetype of the fourth kind of being, the cause of mixing. The mixer is also a measurer.

Certain peculiarities in Plato's presentation suggest, however, that it is motivated by the developments in ancient measurement theory that I have described. First of all, the distinction made between the limited and the unlimited is virtually analytic. This would not be necessary for a distinction between number and magnitude, because of the phenomenon of commensurability. But the class of the more and the less, the pair which characterizes the unlimited, is said to disallow the existence of definite quantity; if it were to allow quantity (ποσόν) and the mean (τὸ μέτριον) to be generated in the seat of its domain (ἕδρᾳ ἐγγενέσθαι), the more-and-less themselves (a dual subject in Plato's Greek) would be made to wander from the place where they properly exist (24c-d). The class of the unlimited therefore stands for the greater-and-less *qua* greater and less, those magnitudes which refuse numerical measurement of any kind, like the radically incommensurable lengths (commensurable neither in length nor in square). The class of the limited, on the other hand, is said to cover only those things which admit of everything opposite to the more-and-less (τούτων δὲ τὰ ἐναντία πάντα δεχόμενα):

πρῶτον μὲν τὸ ἴσον καὶ ἰσότητα, μετὰ δὲ τὸ ἴσον τὸ διπλάσιον καὶ πᾶν ὅτιπερ ἂν πρὸς ἀριθμὸν ἀριθμὸς ἢ μέτρον ᾖ πρὸς μέτρον ...   (25a-b)

first the equal and equality, and after the equal the double and everything whatever which is a number in relation to a number or a measure to a measure.

The limited is therefore the class of commensurable magnitude. Is the distinction between limited and unlimited then a descriptive one based on that between number and magnitude, or really an analytic one between two kinds of magnitude, the commensurable and the incommensurable?

The mixed class is also described as the class (ἰδέα) of the equal and the double (25d); this means it must be meant to include within it the whole class of the limited or commensurable. One could have expected this if it corresponds to a class of scalable magnitudes. But why distinguish this class at all? Socrates goes on to add this curious category to its domain:

... καὶ ὁπόση παύει πρὸς ἄλληλα τἀναντία διαφόρως ἔχοντα, σύμμετρα δὲ καὶ σύμφωνα ἐνθεῖσα ἀριθμὸν ἀπεργάζεται.   (25d-e)

also so much of a class as stops things which are opposites, differently disposed to one another, and fashions them into things commensurable and harmonious by putting in number.

This function appears to be unique to the mixed kind of being. Since only incommensurable things can be made commensurable, the unlimited did indeed signify the incommensurable, as was surmised; and the class mixed from the limited and the unlimited appears to include a new species not found in either apart, which makes incommensurable magnitudes commensurable by 'putting in' or 'inserting' (ἐντίθημι) number. With somewhat uncharacteristic acuity, Protarchus understands Socrates to mean that certain constructions (or 'generations', γενέσεις) follow from the mixing of the Pythagorean opposites (25e). (This interchange seems to be a single Platonic exposition split between two speakers. The author better remembers his dramatic premises when, within less than a Stephanus page, he has Protarchus suddenly express his unsureness about what Socrates could have meant by the members of the third class.)

The two ways of measuring magnitude in terms of a single unit length, by means of a number or an indeterminate dyad of numbers, correspond to the two classes which make up Socrates' third category. In particular, the second way of measuring corresponds to that construction described above which is unique to the mixed category. Both take up magnitudes that were formerly irreconcilable, subsumed by an opposition of greater to less—that is, incommensurables belonging to

the category of the unlimited—and make them
concordant and commensurable by 'inserting number'.
But neither of them does this in such a way as thereby to
reduce these magnitudes to the class of the limited.
Rather, certain lengths turn up in the measurement of
magnitude, incommensurable as such but commensurable
in square, which call forth a peculiar application of
number, one that inserts greater and lesser values in such
a way that they become more and more equal. This use of
numbers comes to light only in measurement science, and
hence only in the mixed category of beings; it does not
suggest itself in the operations of pure arithmetic, the
science of the class of the limited (governing numerable,
discrete quanta and their formal equivalents, like
commensurable lengths). An indeterminate dyad is a
numerical description of a peculiar kind of length, neither
irrational nor rational, but belonging to a third analytic
class called 'expressible' in Euclid.

The mathematical subtext of Socrates' proposal
therefore runs as follows: the distinction between
unlimited, limited, and mixed *is*, after all, a descriptive

one based on that between magnitude, number, and measured magnitude. But when Socrates attempts to bring unity to each category, drawing together into one (εἰς ἕν, 25a, 25d, etc.) the beings subsumed by each, he employs a three-part analytic distinction that applies properly to magnitude alone. That is to say, he brings unity to each of the three realms—magnitude, number, and measured magnitude—by describing each of them in terms of the particular kind of length, the particular kind of one-dimensional magnitude, which uniquely characterizes it. (Perhaps we should think of length, number, and the modernly familiar 'number line'.) Hence the class of the unlimited is not just the class of the greater-and-less, but the class which positively rejects numerical description, like that of the radically incommensurable lengths. (The analogy is strict, for recall that this class is said to reject from its own rightful seat both definite quantity (ποσόν) and the mean (τὸ μέτριον); on my reconstruction, this means it rejects the only two ways of counting lengths, either with a single number, or with an indeterminate dyad of numbers that approximate

a geometric mean.) The class of the limited, likewise, is
not just the class of numerable things, things which can be
expressed as ratios of a number to a number, but also the
class of certain kinds of magnitude, those which can be
expressed as ratios of a measure to a measure, for
commensurable lengths share all the properties of
numbers. Hence the distinction between magnitude and
number (unlimited and limited) can be reduced to a
distinction between two kinds of line. And finally, the
mixed class, or the class of the scale, though it includes
within it the class of the limited, comes to be
characterized by a use of numbers and a kind of
magnitude which are each unique to it. These are the
indeterminate dyad and the lengths which it measures,
once incommensurable but now made 'expressible' by the
insertion of number. The expressible roots form a third
analytic possibility within the field of one-dimensional
extension, alongside rational and irrational lines.
Irrational lines are incommensurable both in length and
in square; rational lines are commensurable both in length
and in square; and expressible lines are incommensurable

in length, but commensurable in square.

The reductionist spirit of Socrates' analysis is in the best traditions of ancient mathematics. To reduce one problem to another is of course heuristic of a solution, but the process can also be useful in definitions and classifications. An example has been given in Aristotle's reduction of the problem of squaring to that of finding a mean proportional line. One effect of Euclid's proposition II.14, which contains a solution to Aristotle's reduced problem, is in turn to reduce a comparison in magnitude between any rectilinear figures to a comparison between squares, and hence to a comparison in one dimension, between square roots. A later and particularly virtuosic example is to be found in Apollonius' use of the three kinds of application of area upon lines, the parabolic, hyperbolic, and elliptic, to both name and define the three kinds of conic section. In Plato's case, the distinctions between his ontological realms of the unlimited, limited, and mixed—two of which, as opposites, had had a long-standing currency in metaphysical thinking—have been reduced to the distinctions between the three kinds of line studied in the new measurement science.

This analysis is also in the spirit of the 'enumerative' method Socrates had earlier set out (16c-17a). One is to seek out the form (ἰδέα) which lends unity to a field of phenomena, and then seek out those things measured by this hypothetical unit-form (i.e., those phenomena which are 'numbers' if the original form is taken as a unit). The method intends to be self-correcting, for one is enjoined in turn to analyse the original unit (τὸ κατ' ἀρχὰς ἕν, 16d) in the same way that one has analysed the enumerated phenomena, to see 'how many' it might actually be. A converse procedure is equally espoused in the case of a science like grammar (18a-d): when the datum seems unlimited or continuous, as does the phenomenon of human vocalization, one is first to discover the *numbers* into which it naturally divides, which govern pluralities such as those marked out by the distinction between vowels and consonants, before one proceeds to analyse these further into their units. There may be an analogy here with modern analyses in terms of 'sets', which also presume that things need to be sorted before they can be counted or related. Euclid's definition of ratio (V.3) requires a relation of kind between the compared terms. Even the infinite field of number itself is nowadays divided in such a way that unitary types may be distinguished ('Reals' over 'Rationals' and 'Irrationals') while individual members remain both infinite and infinitely instantiatable.

An 'enumerative theory of forms' would seem to reflect the ontological and epistemological implications of the interdependence of sorting, on the one hand, and counting or measuring on the other. The new Socratic method is developed as an explicit reaction to the Parmenidean or Pythagorean type of thinker—but also, perhaps, to the early Plato—who analyses everything in terms of opposed principles like the one and the many or the limited and the unlimited, and fails to articulate the crucial phenomena that are ordered, like numbers, in between such opposites. Hasty and simplistic analysis in terms of opposites is said to characterize arguments that are made eristically, while the enumerative method, the method that discovers the numbers of things and their ordered relations, characterizes the truly dialectical approach (17a).

Socrates had earlier made it clear (14d-15c) that the familiar paradoxes of the one and the many were no longer his concern. Any lazy riddler could prove that an individual like Protarchus, or a thing made up of parts, was at the same time one and many. It was the possibility of *formal* unity, in the face of the sensible births and deaths of numberless individuals, the unity that is asserted of things in discourse—whether of 'man' or of 'ox' or of the beautiful or the good—that was of vital philosophical interest. Did any such units exist? How might *they* persist as individuals? And how is it that they partake of the infinite multiplicity of things that come into being? The genuineness of these perplexities calls forth his enumerative approach, a philosophical pathway that Socrates says he had ever loved, but which had often deserted him in the past (16b). The method is hard, but the results can apparently be astonishing; *all* the achievements of the arts (τέχναι) are said to have been discovered on this road (16c).

The implications of this method, shot through as it is with the influence of the burgeoning measurement science, are staggering for the 'classical' Plato. Consider that we are here hypothesizing the existence of forms as measures, enumerating phenomena in terms of a posited unit-form, and then examining the posited unit, presumably against the phenomena themselves, to check for its possible plurality. The method itself is therefore mixed, in such a way as to cancel Plato's earlier formulations. Neither is this the unhypothetical reasoning from forms to forms, whatever that may have meant in *The Republic*, nor is it a reasoning from unquestioned hypotheses, in the manner of synthetic geometry. The once eternal forms, the objects and immutable guarantors of knowledge, have become provisional and heuristic.

God is said to have made all beings out of the one and the many with the limited and the unlimited as innate possessions (16c). This would tend to insure that all phenomena will be inherently numerable, and hence to guarantee their susceptibility to an enumerative method; we shall find the unifying form, for it is in there (εὑρήσειν γὰρ ἐνοῦσαν, 16d). It is as though the pairs of opposed ontological elements, once the principles of the eristic disputations, have now been 're-packaged' in the premises, made the condition for the possibility of an enumerable reality. Inasmuch as it was Aristotle's understanding (*Metaphysics* M.4, 1078b12) that the theory of forms was invented in the first place to account for our sense of dependable knowledge in the face of a Heraclitean flux—and note that the premise of a reality in flux is still accepted at *Philebus* 43a—it seems that this theory has now been modified to make sense not so much of our ability to know as of our ability to count. And this change of purpose is sparked in turn by a renewed confidence in this sovereign ability, in light of Theaetetus' successful attack on the irrational. Number had at last been restored to some of her Pythagorean glory, as a measure of the things that are, that they are, and the things that are not, that they are not, and what is more, of the things *in between*.

The victory here was sweet indeed, for the irrational square roots were recovered from the domain of flux and incommensurability on the very terms by which this domain is distinguished. The indeterminate dyad is both a measurement and a *process* of measurement: interpolating means between means involves a measurer and a thing measured which are continually changing, just as in the Heraclitean or Protagorean contentions; yet this process of itself yields a unique measure of the fixed mean proportional *between* the interpolated means, and makes expressible and commensurable the once irrational root of a rectangular number.

Indeed, this process of measuring or counting in an indeterminate dyad has proved to be revelatory of form, in the sense that it creates the class of the expressible and defines the mixed category of being. On the one hand, things need to be sorted before they can be counted, and hence the knowledge of form has primacy over measurement, and the ability to count depends upon the ability to know. But it would seem in this case that the act of measurement can itself be disclosive of form, and hence that knowing can depend on counting. There appears therefore to be a dialectical relationship between sorting and counting, which is reflected in a self-correcting, enumerative theory of forms. This methodology of the *Philebus* can be seen as reincorporating certain aspects of the Pythagorean, in the sense that once again, knowledge has become coordinated with measurement, and to know something is in some sense to comprehend its number.

Confidence in the grounds of an enumerative approach to the sensible world—a confidence that may once have deserted Socrates in the face of an irrational diameter, leading him, with Meno's honest slave, to the abyss of irony—can allow that significant guarantees of veracity will come from the method itself. There are, for example, different ways to 'count' or measure a phenomenon, each of them legitimate, based on the premises and aims of the investigator, as the several alternate divisions of the sophist and the statesman make clear. One measure of the truth of a hypothesis, that such-and-such a form is a genuine unit, must, under this method, be the economy and scope of the enumeration it affords, *as* a unit in fact. A criterion for a successful articulation, a guarantor that a dialectical enumeration corresponds to a real one in the world, must therefore be the *elegance* of that articulation, in terms of the economy of means and breadth of cover which problem-solving mathematicians have always striven for in the concrete practice of their art.

Indeed, it is an informed sense of respect for developments and concrete formulations in the arts that seems to move the older Plato. In the spheres of grammar and music, for example, although it appears that an abstract analysis in terms of opposites, in the manner of the σοφοί, may to some extent be applied in the interpretation of phenomena, by itself it simply does not make you much of a useful theorist (17b-c). An investigation into the numbers and kinds of sounds, on the other hand, or an enumeration of the different scales and modes and the vagaries of rhythm—these, it seems, can truly render you wiser than the common run, in music and in grammar.

Behind this sensitivity of Plato's to the enumerative and the concrete aspects of the arts, as against the approach through dogmatic first principles, may rest his experience of the dramatic changes in the mathematics of his day. A distinction like that between the rational and the irrational, which must have seemed as basic to the science as that between odd and even numbers—an eternal, immutable opposition, seemingly a part and principle of the order of things—was made obsolete by the emergence into history of a new formulation through the mind of a single, brilliant practitioner.

Recall that Theaetetus' reforms began very humbly on the level of classification and definition: he makes the distinction between square and non-square the basic one for number, beyond the distinctions between, say, odd and even or prime and composite. But of itself this suggests a new way to approach the measurement of lengths, as geometric means, and this further yields, or reveals, a third, formally distinct category of magnitude eventually called 'expressible'. Experiencing this revolutionary development, as witness or participant, must lead a thinker away from a view of τὰ μαθηματικά as eternal, innate verities that can be investigated and learned as though by recollection, towards a view of mathematics that must acknowledge the importance and ingenuity of the problem-solver *in situ*, together with the power of classifications, definitions and measurements to reveal, or to obscure, the fundamental nature of their objects. As the traditional theory of forms and the doctrine of μάθησις ἀνάμνησις ('learning is recollection') can be seen as responding to the ontology and epistemology of the earlier geometry, so can a self-correcting, enumerative theory of forms be seen as a response to the ontological and epistemological implications of the new mathematics and a dynamic measurement science.

Insofar as other arts aspire to the mathematical, the new philosophical outlook must also apply to them; although, to be fair, the provisional, enumerative approach would have long since guided the formulations of practitioners in music and grammar, without a felt need for a mathematical paradigm or a philosopher's blessing. Perhaps one should credit Plato only with waking up to the new realities of science and art around him, much in the spirit of later revolutions in philosophy. One need not qualify, however, one's estimate of the implications of this change of view for Plato's political thought; they are as great as the differences between the *Republic* and the *Laws*. In this vein, while Plato's guardians had learnt their lessons and then interpreted the world, so that nature and politics alike would have been for them a kind of applied mathematics, Plato's statesman is of an altogether different mould of mathematician. He is a problem solver, in amongst it like a navigator or a physician, who must be able to adapt his laws to suit changing conditions, or improve upon his formulations to serve the present (see *Politicus* 295c ff., 300c). It is of course notorious that the guardians' inability to solve a problem,—the numbering of love, and its irrational quantities—leads inexorably to the degeneration of their regime.

C. *Aristotle and the Academy*

In *Metaphysics* N, Aristotle introduces his redaction and criticism of the Platonist (or Academic) metaphysics with this statement: 'All thinkers make the principles opposites' (πάντες δὲ ποιοῦσι τὰς ἀρχὰς ἐναντίας, 1087a30). There appear to have been various schools of thought among Academic ontologists, all of whom posited the unit as a first principle or 'element', but each of whom disagreed as to the nature of the opposite principle, whether it was the 'greater-and-less' or the 'unequal' or 'plurality'. Aristotle makes short shrift of all these formulations, as they treat affections and attributes and relative terms as substances (1088a16). In N.2, he mentions a group who posit the indeterminate dyad as the opposed element, as a way of getting around some difficulties in the other versions; but it is still a relative principle, and in addition, all these formulations fall to Aristotle's argument that eternal things simply cannot be composed of elements (1088b28-35).

Aristotle then feels, before he adumbrates his own approach to ontology, that he must explain why these thinkers ever came up with formulations so narrow and forced, constrained as they are by the dogma of opposed principles (1088b35 ff.). His answer is that they had framed the problem of ontological multiplicity in an old-fashioned way (ἀρχαϊκῶς, 1089a1-2), for they were still arguing in response to certain paradoxes of Parmenides.

The implications of this reconstruction of recent intellectual history are decisive both for our sense of Aristotle's access to Plato, and for our knowledge of Academic thought and *its* relation to Plato. *All* the Academics, and thus Plato as well, are said to reason about existence in terms of an opposed pair of first principles— always the unit and something else; they do this under the direct influence of Parmenides, perhaps as part of a tradition of arguing against certain eristic dogmas of his, such as the one Aristotle quotes in hexameter:

οὐ γὰρ μήποτε τοῦτο δαμῇ, εἶναι μὴ ἐόντα　(1089a4)

For this may never be enforced, that things which
are not, are.

These thinkers are said to have felt that the possibility of
multiplicity in the world would be threatened unless
Parmenides were refuted, and some other thing than
unity or being were allowed to exist. This was the origin of
the 'relative' principles that stood opposite the unit. The
unit and the indeterminate dyad, on this scheme of
Aristotle's, are but one alternative among several pairs of
first principles proposed by different Academic
philosophers.

The first thing to note is that the *Philebus* itself is
Plato's direct and unambiguous criticism of the
ontological reasoning based on two opposed principles, in
favour of a technical, empirical, enumerative approach.
From the perspective of philosophical method, the
dialogue can hardly be said to have any other point. Plato
conceived of his enumerative method as a more
illuminating and more useful way of articulating
phenomena, which comes to yield significant new

categories in the analysis of being (e.g., the mixed one and the cause of mixing). No further clue seems to be necessary for the conclusion: Aristotle, somehow or another, has entirely missed the point of Plato's late formulations, by classing them with the type that Plato himself characterizes as eristic rather than dialectical, and from which he most particularly wants to distinguish his own.

The next point, however, is that there must actually have been a vigorous tradition of thought which both preceded Plato and outlasted him *in his own Academy*, characterized by the use of opposites as first principles. To believe so much is the only way to attach any seriousness to Aristotle's redaction. This tradition originates with Parmenides, and must once have included Plato in its ranks, again if one is to pay any respect to Aristotle's judgement. But Plato came to argue against such thinkers not only in the *Philebus*, but also in the *Sophist*, where they are called 'the friends of the forms' (οἱ τῶν εἰδῶν φίλοι, 248a). These were the latter-day champions of eternal, immutable, unmixing forms, the kind of weary theoretical construct that is often now taught as Platonism. When the differences seem so clear, the question must become: how could Plato's new 'mixed' ontology have come to be confused with the old-fashioned approach through polar principles?

Recall that on my reading of the *Philebus*, there are for Plato three ontological realms apart from the agent of cause. The first is the realm of the limit, the realm of arithmetic, whose principle is the unit. The second is the realm of the unlimited; its principle, analytically opposed to the unit, is the dual greater-and-less, the principle of irrational flux. The third realm is that of the mixed beings, the realm of measurable things. Its principles are two, and reflect the two ways that magnitudes may be numbered or made commensurable, absolutely in terms of the unit or relatively by an indeterminate dyad. The thing to note is that the unit appears as a principle twice in this scheme, opposed in *two different ways* to *two different things*. The distinction between the unit and the greater-and-less is strictly analytic, and belongs squarely in the Parmenidean tradition; whereas the distinction between the unit and the indeterminate dyad is merely descriptive, serving to recognize ways of applying numbers inside the sphere of magnitudinal measurement that happen not to arise in pure arithmetic. The unit and the dyad are therefore not opposites; they are simply different.

If a thinker in the Parmenidean tradition, or a historian of the Parmenidean tradition, were to interpret Plato's scheme in light of their own practices, or to force it into a Parmenidean mould to flatter a historical premise, the conflation of the two distinctions would be an inevitable result. If the *Philebus* could not be consulted—if it were ἄγραφος in the sense 'unpublished'—no recourse could be had to the original reasoning; but even if there were such recourse, Plato's three realms of number, magnitude, and measure, and the important differences between the distinctions unit/greater-and-less and unit/ indeterminate dyad, could only be understood in light of an underlying mathematical paradigm, as I have argued. Such a thinker or such an historian would not be likely to know or to care about the analytic possibilities in one dimension. (This is as much as to say, he would not know what was meant by the indeterminate dyad.) He will look for the polar principles in any ontological scheme; at best he will see that the indeterminate dyad must connote something different from the greater-and-less, as the principle chosen to stand opposite the unit. But he will never envision a scheme that encompasses *both* oppositions.

The question next to ask is whether it was his Academic sources, or whether it was Aristotle himself who did not understand the mathematical meaning of the indeterminate dyad. There is intriguing evidence in *Metaphysics* M and N for the latter interpretation. It would seem that his sources were in the dark about this too; but whatever one concludes about the Academy, there is evidence that Aristotle had Plato's accounts at hand either to quote or to paraphrase, and that he could not make sense of them.

In N.1 (1087b7 ff.), Aristotle mentions a group of thinkers who attempt to generate the numbers from the 'unequal dyad of the great and small', taken as a material principle in relation to the formal 'one', and someone else

who would generate them from the principle of plurality.
(He probably intends, respectively, the followers of Plato
and Speusippus.)[31] The generation of numbers does not
seem to have been a concern of Plato's, however; the
'problem' of multiplicity, or of how things can be both one
and many, which when posed by Parmenides might have
led his successors to theorize in the abstract about the
generating of numbers, seems to be regarded in the
Philebus (14c-15a, 16c-17a) as merely a staple of the eristic
paradoxes, now subsumed within the premises of
Socrates' concrete enumerative approach. Which is to say,
it appears that Plato is no longer so interested in number
theory as he is in simply *counting*. I am therefore inclined
to think that neither the above-mentioned group nor the
'someone else' represents Plato's line of argument, or
Plato's understanding of the unequal dyad.

Aristotle bears this out by going on immediately to
mention an *individual* who speaks of the one and the
unequal dyad as ontological elements (1087b9), thereby

---

[31]Julia Annas, *Aristotle's* Metaphysics *Books M and N*, Oxford: Oxford
University Press, 1976, 195

distinguishing him from the group who had used them (afterwards, I presume) as formal and material elements in the generation of numbers. Aristotle's complaint about this individual is that he does not make the distinction that the unequal dyad of great and small is one thing in formula (λόγῳ), but not in number (ἀριθμῷ).

Why would not Plato have made this distinction? The unequal dyad is not one thing in formula alone: the successive pairs of interpolated numbers relate uniquely to *one object* as well, the side of the square that is their single geometric mean. Further, since it consists of successively more equal sides of a single rectangular number, the dyad can quite emphatically and strikingly be said to be *of one number*, with a rationale that Aristotle might have appreciated if he had been more familiar with the construction.

On this model of progressively 'equalized' rectangular numbers, we have a transparent motivation for the original formulation of terms like 'unequal', 'indeterminate dyad', 'greater-and-lesser', and 'exceeding and exceeded', which find their way into the theories of

Plato's followers. In addition—and this point would seem to be decisive for the interpretation—we should expect to find them opposed in this context to a concept of the unit which is associated with the square or 'equal'. On no other grounds but those of the new measurement science, as I have described them here, would such an association be expected. Sure enough, the unit in these theories is described as the equal (1087b5, 1092b1), in such a way as to mystify not only Aristotle but also modern interpreters of these passages.[32]

Neither Aristotle nor his Academic sources seem to connect these various expressions with geometrical representations of number; the theories on the generation of numbers betray no influence of Theaetetus' square/oblong distinction, nor of the geometrical interpretation of number that is settled convention by the time of Euclid. The Academics seem to have posited 'ideal' numbers which were generated individually in succession (two, three, four, as Aristotle says in M.7 1081a23, and so without distinction as to square or oblong) from the unit

---

[32]Ibid.

and the indeterminate dyad. Aristotle takes some pains to make sense of this theory: if the units (monads) of ideal numbers are all the same and addible, then they are not ideal at all, but normal mathematical numbers (cf. 1081a19); but if the monads of each ideal number are distinct and inaddible, they must be generated *before* each of their respective numbers can be generated, as a point of logic (1081a26 ff.). This is true no matter how these monads are generated; but Aristotle once more quotes 'he who first said it' (ὁ πρῶτος εἰπών, 1081a24)—again distinguishing him from those who later used such phrases as the 'unequal dyad'—to allude to a possible mechanism for this generation of inaddible monads (ἀσύμβλητοι μονάδες): they arise out of unequals, once these are equalized (ἐξ ἀνίσων (ἰσασθέντων γὰρ ἐγένοντο)).

To begin with, Aristotle cannot rightly make attribution to *anyone* of a theory on the generation of inaddible monads. As he says, no one actually spoke that way (1081a36). Aristotle, perhaps himself in reaction against the eristic movement, constructs these arguments to save his opponents from the obvious fallacy of *ideal* numbers composed of normal, identical, addible monads; yet the alternative, unstated by them, but which he says follows reasonably from their own premises, turns out to be impossible as well, if truth be told (1081b1). There is therefore no reason to suppose that Plato thought or said that the generation of inaddible monads, or any monads, was connected with his notion of the unequal. On the contrary; Plato seems to have anticipated Aristotle's notion of the unit as a measure, both in the intuitions of the enumerative method and in the specifically mathematical context. At 57d-e, the distinction is made in the *Philebus* between the units of the arithmetic of the many, which change as different things are counted, and those of the arithmetic of the philosophizers, which are always identical. It would of course have been an easy (but pointless) solution to the problem of the irrational to say that incommensurables are simply measured by different unit lengths than commensurables. The enumeration of Theaetetus and Plato, on the other hand, is predicated on the assumption of identical units. While some lengths still remain incommensurable on these terms, all the formerly irrational square roots become expressible through an indeterminate dyad, and the achievement of this articulation would be lost without the assumption.

What *can* be attributed to Plato, however, is that his notion of the unequal involved a process of equalizing it. In neither place in M where Aristotle mentions this idea (as above, and at 1083b24) can he make anything of it, nor does it seem to have any intuitive connection to the Academic number-generation theories he covers there. The only conclusion, I suggest, is that Aristotle refers to this conception of the unequal merely because he knows it to have been true of Plato's thought. The 'Platonists' speak of the unequal as a generative principle, Aristotle might have reasoned, and who knows what they mean, as to *how* it generates; Plato himself also spoke of the unequal, and the only action he attributed to it was 'being equalized'; perhaps this was somehow the 'generating action', as obscure as that seems; one ought therefore to mention what the old man said, in fairness to them.

In N, Aristotle for the first time mentions a

number-generation theory which did, perhaps, try to interpret the process; it first declares that there is no generation of odd numbers at all, and that the even numbers are generated out of the great and small when these are equalized. Aristotle's criticism of the logic of this account verges on the sarcastic: φανερὸν ὅτι οὐ τοῦ θεωρῆσαι ἕνεκεν ποιοῦσι τὴν γένεσιν τῶν ἀριθμῶν. ('Clearly, it is not on account of philosophical theorizing that they produce their generation of the numbers.' 1091a29) Neither Aristotle, for whom the notion seemed fatuously self-contradictory, nor these latter theorists, for whom it was received dogma, could have known the original mathematical context, for neither could interpret or properly apply the notion that the unequal as an elemental principle involved a process of being equalized. We can now restore the context, in the process of 'equalizing' an unequal, oblong number with an indeterminate dyad of more and more equal rational factors. (It is particularly striking that these latter Academics seemed to know that the notion 'unequal-when-it-is-equalized' served in such a way as to divide all numbers, but they tried, with dismal consequence, to apply it to the familiar, venerable distinction between odd and even; they must have been unaware of the division of numbers by square and oblong, which supplanted the earlier distinction in the course of Theaetetus' study of irrational roots, and where alone the notion of the 'equalized unequal' has any use or coherence.)

'Those who say the unequal is some one thing, making the indeterminate dyad from great and small, say things that are far indeed from being likely or possible,' in Aristotle's view (M.1, 1088a15). He complains that to adopt such ideas is really to adopt his lowly Category of the 'relative' as a substantial, unitary first principle. Something is great or small only in relation to something else. Unlike the superior Categories of quality and quantity, which have more substance because they involve absolute change, whether by alteration or increase, there is no such change proper to the Category of the relative. While a compared term may remain substantially the same, it becomes greater or less merely by quantitative change in the other term. Aristotle is therefore at a loss as to why such metaphysical honour should be paid to concepts that are inherently relative.

Plato could have replied: 'consider the nature of measurement toward the generation of the mean.' In this process, the relative terms do *not* depend simply on each other, but both are related to an unchanging third thing, a single geometric mean. Furthermore, the pairs of relative terms are *uniquely* related to their proper mean, the root of a particular oblong number. And because the greater and lesser lengths approach closer than any given difference to the unchanging length of the root, their status in relation to this length, *qua* members of an infinite succession of approximating pairs, poses a heady puzzle for any common-sense idea of their ontological difference from, or identity with, this single length. There is therefore every reason to see the indeterminate dyad of great and small, a self-correcting binary approximation of a single geometric mean, as a unitary and substantial thing in its proper mathematical context. But if the context was lost, and one had access only to the words in its name, then Aristotle's objections might seem judicious.

That Aristotle knew about the geometry of means is clear enough, but he must not have been familiar with the interpolation of means in the peculiar configuration of the indeterminate dyad, where means become extremes, which in turn beget means, which then in turn become extremes, while *each* pair of harmonic and arithmetic means serves as the extremes to the geometric mean in the middle. The notion of relativity embodied in this configuration, involving a process of equalizing, and motion towards a fixed object, is more subtle and peculiar than that involved in a simple comparison, or even a static analysis expressed in terms of a mean and extremes. I claim it is *this* peculiar conception of the relative that Plato raised to the level of a principle, to stand in tandem with the absolute measure connoted by the unit.

While the Academic metaphysicians may appear to have used these very same principles, right down to the letter of their formulation, it is clear that neither they nor Aristotle grasped their proper function. They have nothing to do with accounting for multiplicity in the universe, or with the generation of numbers. They have everything to do with the *measurement* of numbers. After Theaetetus, numbers are figured as square or rectangular; they can be compared not only in quantity, but in size, by the length of their square roots, just as after Euclid's II.14, any rectilinear figures can be compared by the sides of their equivalent squares. While all numbers have either absolutely or relatively measurable root-lengths, not all lengths have countable squares. This is one of the odd new ways that arithmetic and geometry, number and magnitude, become interlinked after Theaetetus' happy reformulation.

It is therefore in this context, the context of measurement, that Plato is likely to have distinguished the absolute from the relative, being-in-itself from relative being. Aristotle alludes to just such a distinction, in a passage which once again exemplifies his peculiar mire: he wants to review the Academic theories on the generation of multiplicity based on certain contrary principles, including principles first conceived by Plato, but conceived in a context where in some cases they weren't even contraries, and where they had had nothing to do with generating either multiplicity or numbers; he knows the language of Plato's own articulation of these principles, but doesn't have the mathematics to interpret the words. In this case, he may even foist his own innovations in usage back on to Plato's original phrases, just to make sense of them.

At 1089b16, Aristotle once again invokes 'he who says these things', claiming this time that this person had also proved for himself (προσαπεφήνατο) that that which was potentially a 'this' and substance (τὸ δυνάμει τόδε καὶ οὐσία) was not 'existent in itself' (ὂν καθ' αὑτό); it was the 'relative' (τὸ πρός τι). What the expression 'potentially a "this" and substance' may have meant for Plato is a difficult thing to determine. In particular, Aristotle seems to take δυνάμει, with obvious anachronism, in his own characteristic sense of 'potentially'; he had just now used the word this way when introducing part of his own familiar solution to ontological analysis, that we must hypothesize in each case what a thing is potentially (ἀνάγκη μὲν οὖν ... ὑποθεῖναι τὸ δυνάμει ὂν ἑκάστῳ, 1089b15-16). Perhaps Aristotle is here weaving his own terminology into the Platonic materials? But his next comment is a scholium, on Plato's appropriation of the term 'relative', that it is just as if he had said 'quality' (ὥσπερ εἰ εἶπε τὸ ποιόν); and there was never a scholium without a text.

So what could the Greek text 'τὸ δυνάμει τόδε καὶ οὐσία' have meant to Plato? Recall Knorr's observation that δύναμις and δυνάμει mean 'square' and 'in square' throughout Greek mathematical literature.[33] (The only exception is the very passage in the *Theaetetus* [148a] where the eponymous hero applies the term δύναμις, for the first time, to a square root.) Thus in Plato's context, the same words may well have signified 'that which has particularity and existence in square'—that is, that which is countable (because it is commensurable) only in square (δυνάμει), like the expressible as against the rational lines. It is these very magnitudes which one could expect to find distinguished as relative in their being, insofar as their being depends on their measure; the rational lengths, on the other hand, have the self-subsistent being of definite

---

[33]Knorr, *Evolution*, 65-9

quantity, in length and in square, while the irrational lines, which cannot be made commensurable in either length or square, are captive to the realm of flux and non-being. If Plato equated 'that which has being' with 'that which can be counted'—and his enumerative method suggests a move in this direction—then it is entirely and specifically appropriate that that which has being in square be allowed only a relative existence. It has no autonomous number, but only a relative count. Even the phrase πρός τι may have had a specific connotation for Plato, which is lost in the anachronistic aura of the Categories; for such beings are measured by a process that is inherently πρός τι, 'towards something', measurement toward the generation of the mean. Plato's distinction would have been between that which exists or is measured on its own terms (τὸ ὂν καθ' αὑτό)—the equal, the square, and rational lengths—and that which exists or is measured toward something else (τὸ ὂν πρός τι), the unequal being equalized, the rectangle approaching the square, and the indeterminate dyad approximating the mean.

It seems clear that any such significance in these

phrases could never have been allowed to emerge through the schemata of Aristotle's redaction. He explains (1089b4 ff.) that in response to the diversion caused by Parmenides, the philosophers posited the relative and the unequal as the types of opposed principle which, when mated with being and the unit, generated a manifold reality. He points out, however, that neither of these posited principles is in fact the contrary (ἐναντίον) or the negation (ἀπόφασις) of being and unity; each is rather another single nature among the things that exist (μία φύσις τῶν ὄντων). This is also the point of his critical scholium on Plato's use of the phrase πρός τι: the Category 'relative' is no more a legitimate candidate than the Category 'quality' for that contrary and negation of being and the unit which the Academics were supposed to be seeking; each is simply 'some one' of the beings (ἕν τι τῶν ὄντων, 1089b20). He goes on to complain that if Plato had meant to explain how things in general are many, he shouldn't have confined his investigation to things that lie in the same Category (whether this be 'substance' or 'quality' or 'quantity', let alone the insubstantial 'relative').

The sense of this reading ranges from the misguided to the willfully obtuse. In the first instance, we cannot fault Plato for failing either to prophesy or to apply the revolutionary insights into ontology expressed in Aristotle's theory of the Categories. Nor can we fault him for not being interested any longer, as indeed he wasn't, in the problem of how things are many. Still less can we fault him for giving up the reasoning by opposites. He would of course have agreed that his conception of the relative, in the configuration of the indeterminate dyad, is in no sense the opposite of the unit and its measure, but simply a different way of measuring, based also on the unit, that applies to certain types of being (i.e., certain two-dimensional numbers and one-dimensional magnitudes—oblongs and their roots). But the full picture of Aristotle's plight as a redactor emerges when one throws in the fact that Plato's complete formulation *did* in fact include a genuine opposition as well, between the unit and the greater-and-less *qua* greater and less. One then has a recipe for the peculiar quandary of *Metaphysics*

M and N towards Platonic thought, based in part on unwitting conflations, but in part also on flagrant, self-serving anachronisms, and characterized by a haplessness in the face of Plato's own expressions, when read in light of their borrowed use in the irrelevant theories of the Academy.

A question remains: where did Aristotle get those 'texts' of Plato, which he seems to treat as quoted material? Although the distinction between absolute and relative being may be consistent with the *Philebus* and with other ontological discussions in the later Plato, the specific phrases which Aristotle comments on, such as τὸ δυνάμει τόδε καὶ οὐσία, do not seem to occur in the dialogues. Where, then, did Plato draw this mathematical distinction, and to what did he apply it? Was it perhaps in a Lecture on The Good—a lecture which seemed to promise moral philosophy, but delivered mathematics—a lecture which nobody understood?

D. *The Enumerations of Euclid X*

The mathematical development of ancient measurement science will prove much easier to trace than its philosophical obfuscation at the hands of Academics and Peripatetics. As forbidding as the structure of Euclid's *Elements* X seems to be, I believe its logic is profoundly simple, following directly in the spirit of Plato's enumerative method, and upon Theaetetus' geometrical interpretation of number.

After Theaetetus' first efforts had rendered all the square roots countable, he next sought to extend his classificatory net even further into the uncharted regions of the irrational. He could use his already successful methods as a paradigm: since exploring numbers in terms of the means between them had yielded the class of expressible lines, he was led to explore the possibility of means between the expressible lengths themselves, and the possibility of irrational means. While in general such means could not be 'counted off', since the expressible lengths, treated as extremes, had not the fixed values necessary for a computation of means, the mean lengths could still be constructed and named with respect to rational lengths; just as at the time of the *Meno*, the root length of the double square could not as yet be counted, but it could be constructed within the unit square and was named 'diameter' (or the 'through-measure') by the professors (*Meno* 85b). Orders of irrationals could thus be defined in terms of means, though they could not be made commensurable.

Just such an assignment of orders is credited to Theaetetus by Pappus, in his commentary on *Elements* X, on the authority of Eudemus' history of mathematics (now lost):

> ... it was ... Theaetetus ... who divided the more generally known irrational lines according to the different means, assigning the medial line to geometry, the binomial to arithmetic, and the apotome to harmony, as is stated by Eudemus, the

Peripatetic.[34]

The passage does not suggest that Theaetetus invented the three lines and their names, but only that he first saw the essential parallelism between the structure of their relations and those of the familiar means. The medial simply *is* the geometric mean between two expressible lengths. That is why it is called μέση, the mean proportional; the name 'medial' serves only to distinguish it in English. The binomial is a sum of two expressible lengths, and so can be associated with the arithmetic mean, which is half the sum of two rational lengths; but the apotome is merely a difference of expressible lengths, and the connection with the harmonic mean is less obvious. This also comes clear, however, as one recalls the fundamental feature of pairs of arithmetic and harmonic means which makes possible the measurement by an indeterminate dyad: if one applies a rectangle contained by rational extremes to the length of their arithmetic mean, the height of the new rectangle turns out to be the

---

[34]tr. W. Thomson and G. Junge, in Fowler, *Mathematics*, 301

length of their harmonic mean. Euclid's X.112-14 illustrate a significantly parallel property of binomials and apotomes: if one were to apply the same rational rectangle to a length that was known to be a binomial, the height would turn out to be an apotome; further, and curiously enough, the expressible terms of such a binomial and an apotome would be *commensurable with each other*, and in the same ratio. If Theaetetus was responsible for these propositions, he might well have been led to view the binomial and apotome as 'irrational means' between rational extremes, or as irrational factors of an oblong number, counterparts to the rational arithmetic and harmonic means.

It is clear, however, that Euclid's presentation is not designed as a theory of means. The bulk of his 115 propositions in Book X are concerned with enumerating and constructing twelve different kinds of binomial and apotome, making with the medial thirteen types of irrational line; the full list is given by Euclid after Prop. 111, before the proofs that establish the analogy between the binomials and apotomes, and the arithmetic and harmonic means. The rationale for this enumeration becomes more apparent if one considers David Fowler's handy grouping of the propositions:

X1-18: general properties of expressible lines and rectangles,

X19-26: medial lines and rectangles,

X27-35: constructions underlying binomials and apotomes,

X36-41, 42-7, 48-53, 54-9, 60-5, 66-70, & 71-2: blocks of propositions dealing with each of the six types of additive irrational lines. They are described in X36-41 and also, in a different geometrical configuration, in the Second Definitions following X47,

X73-8, 79-84, 85-90, 91-6, 97-102, 103-7, & 108-10: blocks of propositions, parallel to the previous, dealing with each of the six types of subtractive irrational lines. They are described in X73-8 and also, in a different geometrical configuration, in the Third Definitions following X84,

X111-14: the relations between binomials and apotomes,

X115: medials of medials ...[35]

---

[35]Fowler, *Mathematics*, 169-70

As Fowler himself observes, the propositions seem to represent an exploration of the 'simplest operations of adding, subtracting, and squaring pairs of expressibles.'[36] Before Theaetetus classified them in relation to the different rational means, the binomial and apotome may have first been distinguished and defined as part of an investigation of the 'arithmetic' of expressible lengths. An investigator might have said, if we are to understand the expressibles the way we understand numbers—and indeed, numbers are the very paradigms of our understanding—then we must comprehend their arithmetic; what might the manipulations of arithmetic look like when applied to expressible lines?

Whereas the prospect of such an investigation might have daunted the most optimistic of researchers, with its seeming open-endedness and unlimited number of possible cases, Euclid was able, by manipulating squares and rectangles, to organize the infinite additions and subtractions of expressible lengths into six types each.

---

[36]Ibid., 192

Thus Euclid accomplished the first ever rigorous ordering of radically incommensurable lengths, as the sums and differences of expressible ones. One cannot measure these sums and differences as such, and so one cannot 'count off' the irrational lines that are produced; but one *can* number their types, and enumerate their orders.

While the fundamental early propositions of Book X are generally credited to Theaetetus, and the propositions about mean proportionals ('medials') seem to suit his historical and mathematical character, the enumeration of the binomials and apotomes must belong to Euclid. Pappus says that Euclid, following Theaetetus, 'determined ... many orders of the irrationals; and brought to light, finally, whatever of finitude (or definiteness) is to be found in them.'[37] This should naturally refer to his ordering of possible binomials and apotomes, and the enumeration of six corresponding types. Though they do not depend on the proofs involved in Euclid's enumeration, Theaetetus' propositions, about the relations between binomials and apotomes, are then

---

[37]tr. Thomson and Junge, in Fowler, *Mathematics*, 301

placed by Euclid at the end of Book X, so that they can be expressed in terms of that enumeration, and take on a new authority: each pair belongs to one of six sets of ordered pairs of binomials and apotomes whose terms turn out to be commensurable and in the same ratio; each pair consists of corresponding members of one of a finite number of possible combinations of additive and subtractive expressible lengths.

It is possible, then, to trace the genesis of Book X in this way: Theaetetus first extended the insights of measurement toward the generation of the mean by using the three means involved in that science as heuristic paradigms with which to interpret irrational magnitudes. Just as an expressible length is a geometric mean between rational extremes, a medial length is a mean proportional between expressible extremes; and just as arithmetic and harmonic means are pairs of commensurable rational factors of the rectangle contained by the extremes of their interval, binomials and apotomes are pairs of *irrational* factors of the same rectangle. In his investigation of binomials and apotomes, Euclid discovered their classification, and thereby produced an ordering of irrationals in terms of possible types of sum and difference—an arithmetic of expressible lines. This in turn advanced the classificatory scope of Theaetetus' propositions on the relations between binomials and apotomes, when they were placed after Euclid's work, at the end of Book X. While Theaetetus could likely have proved that a rational area applied to a binomial produces an apotome as breadth, and that the terms of these irrational factors are commensurable and in the same ratio, Euclid could now add, as he does in the enunciations of Propositions 112 and 113, that such a binomial and an apotome belong to the *same order*.

David Fowler approaches the book from a different angle, as part of his reconstruction of the ancient mathematics of ἀνθυφαίρεσις. He proposes an *anthyphairetic* theory of ratio, where ratios between quantities are described by counting the number of mutual subtractions which can occur between them: one counts the number of times the lesser subtracts from the greater, then the number of times the remainder can be taken away from the lesser, then the remainder of *that* transaction from the former remainder, and so on; the list of numbers thus produced gives a unique description of the particular ratio. He finds evidence for the historical existence of this approach in several quarters, including a direct allusion in Aristotle's *Topics* to a definition of same ratio as same *antanairesis*[38]; and he sees the peculiar implications of this ratio theory as providing the most economical of many proposed rationales for the total sequence and layout of Euclid's Book II. The most surprising fact he uncovers is a remarkable periodicity that arises in the *anthyphairetic* description of ratios of the form $\sqrt{m}:\sqrt{n}$—that is, ratios of expressible lines.

The achievement of Fowler's work is to have rediscovered, and in some measure to have resurrected in our day, the *other* branch of measurement science, measurement πρὸς ἄλληλα. The periodic repetition of the terms in the otherwise infinite mutual subtraction of expressible quantities would have been the great discovery of this science; as Fowler observes:

---

[38]Fowler, *Mathematics*, 17 ff., and see Aristotle, *Topics* 158b

> Those ratios that can be now completely understood
> and described in finite terms by the *arithmoi* include
> the ratios of the sides of commensurable squares,
> that is the ratios of expressible lines $\sqrt{m}$:$\sqrt{n}$ ...[39]

Note how fitly this parallels the development I have described in the science of measurement toward the generation of the mean: those lengths which can now be uniquely measured in terms of the ἀριθμοί include these same expressible lines, the sides of commensurable squares.

As far as the rationale for Euclid's Book X is concerned, however, Fowler's reconstruction of the mathematics of *anthyphairesis* shows only why the relations between expressible lines would have seemed a thing worth investigating. We gain no insight into the specific form of the book as we have it, into its method and structure in the classification of the irrationals; these are better explained as an integral outgrowth of the new science proposed in Plato's *Politicus*, the science of

---

[39]Ibid., 192

measurement toward the generation of the mean.

This is not just because Theaetetus is said to have classified the irrationals in terms of the different means. Consider that the entire investigative strategy of Book X, including the work I have ascribed to Euclid, is to manipulate squares and rectangles, a manipulation in two dimensions, in such a way as to distinguish and to enumerate the forms of the associated lines.[40] This approach was born with the science of measurement toward the mean, on one fateful day. As he lies dying off-stage, the story is told of how the young Theaetetus, Theodorus' student, on the day of Socrates' appearance in court, divided all numbers between the square and the oblong, and distinguished two kinds of line as the sides of squares equal to each kind of number. The names Theaetetus chose for these two lengths, μῆκος and δύναμις, did not survive, for the implications of a classification by sides of squares made the distinction itself obsolete: both kinds of length would now be called ῥητά, 'expressible', by Euclid. But the technique applied in

---

[40]see Ibid., 190-1

Theaetetus' classification was to direct the exploration of lines to its crowning achievement, in the enumerations of truly irrational species of lines in Euclid's Book X. The modern approach to 'numbers' as solutions to equations sidesteps the problem of incommensurability and yields a different ordering of sets. This now discarded notion 'expressible' is the centrepiece and the key to the ancient enumeration, enshrined in the definitions of Euclid X: there is good reason to believe that its ultimate source was Theaetetus' version of a solution to Theodorus' problem, perhaps on a day after wrestling.

We ought, however late, to acknowledge the dramatist who felt the significance of such a day for history, felt it in a way that must combine the personal and the universal, the historical and the mathematical. Innovations in mathematics must have moved that man at some midpoint in his life, in a way that made even innovation in religion seem a distant charge, a memory of youthful import. We must come to recognize the changes in this chronicler of the human argument, as he took his bearings anew, and found new patterns, enumerative structures, emerging in a discourse that strains sometimes clumsily to keep pace—paradigms of order no longer laid up in heaven, yet resonant, perhaps, with a piece of divinity. His myth of the globe's reversal (*Politicus* 268d-274e) encompasses a deteriorating world, but also a return, through the numbering of its classes and kinds, to the elegance of god's tenure. Let him stand absolved at last of the mystifications of his followers: Plato's own measures, his own mysteries, must finally furnish our count.

Select Glossary

In many respects the ancient Greeks were first on the block, and hence did not have dead languages to draw on when they developed terms of art (if you prefer, 'technical terms', or jargon) for use in mathematics and philosophy. Aristotle in particular virtually requires that one familiarize oneself with his coinages—and I mean familiarize oneself with them, through his usage, rather than etymologize them, as is sometimes misleadingly done. The classical poets, historians, philosophers and orators did not subscribe to some standard lexicon. This can be confusing in philosophy, since the modus of technical writing is fully developed with these astonishing innovators, and yet the key terms are not 'done into Greek and Latin,' in the style of, say, Immanuel Kant; usually they are everyday words that in other contexts retain their everyday meanings, often deployed idiosyncratically author by author, and yet technically, if that can be conceived to be possible.

Consider κέντρον, for example; it means 'goad', or 'stinger'—any sort of torturous pointy thing. But in geometry it is a word we do not translate, but rather transliterate as 'centre'. Now, consider what single word one might come up with in English to express this idea, without using 'centre' itself. As for me, I find the problem impossible, and one must be impressed by the people who christened the most central of concepts when, upon reflection, they first called those peculiar geometrical points 'stingers'.

What follows is a brief list of Greek words cited in this study, with a broad-brushed adumbration of their everyday meaning followed by various 'technical' senses. I have not included cases like μῆκος, whose senses pretty well correspond to the various senses of 'length' in English.

ἄλογος, -ον: *stupid, without reason, irrational*; in mathematics, *without ratio, incommensurable, irrational*.

ἀναλογίζειν: whence our 'analogy', but usually in a mathematical context in ancient Greek; to *calculate*, specifically to *solve proportions*.

ἀνθυφαίρεσις, ἀνταναίρεσις: i n mathematics, *reciprocal subtraction*, which leads to the greatest common measure (factor, common denominator) of the original numbers or magnitudes. If the magnitudes are incommensurable, the process goes on forever, but in the case of √m : √n, where m and n are rational, the sequence of numbers counting the successive subtractions begins to repeat *ad infinitum* (David Fowler).

ἀόριστος: *without limit, indeterminate, undefined*; in grammar, *timeless aspect* ('aorist').

ἀποφαίνειν: *show forth, display, declare*; in mathematics, *demonstrate, prove.*

γένεσις: *generation, origin, birth, coming-to-be*; in mathematics, *generation of a figure, construction.*

γράφειν: *write, draw, scratch, ordain* (law); in mathematics, *prove with the use of a figure* (Wilbur Knorr).

δύναμις: *power, ability, force*; in Aristotle, *potential*, **δυνάμει** (dat.) *in potential*; in mathematics, *square, in square*; Theaetetus in *Theaetetus*, *expressible square root* (mod. irrational)

ἐπίτριτον: 'over three'; *ratio 4:3*

ἔχειν λόγον: *have a point, be reasonable, be backed*

by an argument, be rational; in mathematics, *have a ratio, be rational.*

ἡμιόλιον: 'half-and-whole'; *ratio 3:2.*

θεωρεῖν: *consult an oracle, be ambassador to a festival, sight-see, observe*; in philosophy, *contemplate, speculate by means of theory.*

μέσος, μέση: *middle, moderate, in the midst, etc.*; in mathematics and philosophy, *mean, mean proportional.* In Euclid, 'binomial' is literally 'out of two names' (ἐκ δύο ὀνομάτων), perhaps because the thing is formed by addition; 'apotome' (ἀποτομή, *a cutting off, section, scion, etc.*) is likely deployed because formed by subtraction.

μέτριον: *average, moderate, harmonious*; in Plato, *aesthetic, moral,* or *mathematical proportion.*

ὁμοίωσις: *being made 'like', simile*; **ὅμοιον/ ἀνόμοιον**: *like/unlike*; in geometry, *similar* (in proportion and shape)/*dissimilar*; in arithmetic, *square/non-square.*

ὁρίζειν: *set boundary marks, delimit*; in philosophy

and mathematics, *define.*

οὐσία: *substance (wealth)*; in philosophy, *substance, being.*

πρόβλημα: *projection, obstacle, bulwark, excuse*; in philosophy and mathematics, *problem.*

ῥητόν/ἄρρητον: *stated, utterable/unspoken, unutterable, secret, forbidden, sacred, horrible.* In mathematics, *rational, expressible/irrational.*

στοιχεῖον: *simplest sound of speech, letter, physical element, gnomon shadow*; in mathematics, *element of proof.*

συλλαμβάνειν (συλλαβή): *join together, seize, take part in, cooperate with, comprehend, combine; syllable* (composed of elements; note that 'el-em-en' refers to the first three letters of the second column of a Roman schoolboy's exercises).

σύμμετρον: *commensurate with, in step, moderate, in due proportion, symmetrical*; in mathematics, *commensurable.*

Scholarly References

ANNAS, JULIA, *Aristotle's* Metaphysics *Books* M *and* N. Oxford: Oxford University Press, 1976.

BROWN, MALCOLM, '*Theaetetus*: Knowledge as Continued Learning'. *Journal of the History of Philosophy,* 1969, 7:359-79.

BURNYEAT, MILES F, 'The Philosophical Sense of Theaetetus' Mathematics'. *Isis*, 1978, 69:489-513

DAVID, A. P., *The Dance of the Muses: Choral Theory and Ancient Greek Poetics.* Oxford: Oxford University Press, 2006.

FOWLER, DAVID H., *The Mathematics of Plato's Academy.* Oxford: Clarendon Press, 1987.

KNORR. WILBUR R., *Evolution of the Euclidean Elements.* Dordrecht and Boston: D. Reidel Pub. Co., 1975.

——— and MILES F. BURNYEAT, 'Methodology, Philology, and Philosophy'. *Isis*, 1979, 70:565-70

CPSIA information can be obtained
at www.ICGtesting.com
Printed in the USA
FSOW02n0928281117
41743FS